HOW TO
NON-FICTION

Other Allison & Busby Writers' Guides

HOW TO WRITE NON-FICTION BOOKS

Gordon Wells

a&b

This edition published in Great Britain in 1996 by
Allison & Busby
an imprint of Wilson & Day Ltd
179 King's Cross Road
London WC1X 9BZ

First published by The Macmillan Press Ltd/Papermac in 1981 as
The Successful Author's Handbook

Reprinted 1982, 1983, 1984, 1986
Second edition published 1989

A catalogue record for this book is available from
the British Library.

ISBN 0 74900 277 8

Designed and typeset by N-J Design Associates
Romsey, Hampshire
Printed and bound in Great Britain by
WBC Book Manufacturers Ltd, Bridgend, Mid Glamorgan

NOTE

An earlier version of this book, entitled *The Successful Author's Handbook*,
was published by Macmillan Publishers Ltd in 1981 and 1989.
This new Allison & Busby edition, *How to Write Non-fiction Books*, while
building on the same organisational framework and following the same
principles as the earlier book, has been almost completely rewritten.   It
has been broadened to include advice on all types of non-fiction books,
expanded to bring in the benefits of the author's subsequent experience
and modernised to include up-to-date equipment
and procedures.

CONTENTS

INTRODUCTION

Many long to write a book. They dream of having a book on their shelves, with their name on the cover.

Too many dream of that book being a novel. The competition for publication of a first novel is fierce. And it's not as easy as it looks, to tell a good – and commercially viable – story. Few earn the vast sums reported as paid to the big names in popular fiction. But there are also non-fiction books.

Tens of thousands of new books are published each year in Britain alone. Sixty, seventy, eighty thousand new books each year – and rising. And the proportion of non-fiction to fiction is at least five or six to one. There are more opportunities for non-fiction books than there are for novels ... and the competition is not quite so fierce as it is for the aspiring novelist.

Novels – but seldom the really popular ones – attract literary and critical attention; so too do biographies. Other than the most popular – or prestigious, which is not synonymous – novels though, non-fiction books are often better commercial successes.

Many first novels will barely sell a couple of thousand copies; few first novels are taken up by book clubs, paperback publishers and film producers – which is where the big money comes from. Many novelists fade into obscurity, disheartened – and maybe broke – after their first novel. But the greatest best-seller of all time is the Bible – and that is (largely) non-fiction. P. A. Samuelson's classic *Economics* (McGraw-Hill) has sold several million copies, worldwide, in a dozen or so editions and translations. And coming down to earth, most non-fiction books – particularly those of a 'how to' nature – can expect to sell several thousand copies. Two of mine have sold well over ten thousand copies each.

Writing a non-fiction book is every bit as worthy an occupation as writing a novel – and is more likely to achieve success. Many specialists and academics think about writing a book on their subject, as do some hobbyists and amateur historians. Indeed, the career of an upwardly mobile academic will often hinge on his work being published. Many *dream* of producing a non-fiction book on their subject; few actually get down to working on it; fewer still complete the task. It entails a lot of hard work. And there is a right way and a wrong way to go about it.

This book will tell you how to do it the right way.

The professional approach

The first thing to learn is that you will almost certainly have to write your book the way a publisher wants it, which may not be the way you first think of it.

It is often advantageous for a non-fiction book to fit into a publisher's existing series. It may need to be written to a specific length or directed at a slightly different readership from the one you propose. It is therefore important not to start writing your book yet. That's so important, it's worth repeating, and emphasising:

DON'T START WRITING YOUR BOOK YET

A non-fiction book has to be carefully planned; its content needs to be organised; you even need to think about the eventual layout of the book pages. In all these matters, it is best to sound out the views and requirements of the eventual publisher before doing too much writing. It is wisest to adopt a professional approach. The approach is relevant to all forms of non-fiction writing; any minor variations will be touched on later in this introductory chapter.

The professional approach to non-fiction book writing can be thought of as ten steps:

1 Define the SUBJECT of your book. Bear in mind your own knowledge and experience, your ability to cover the whole

subject (or redefine it such that you can) and your ability to gain access to the material you will need.

2 Assess the MARKET for the book. Clarify in your mind the readership you hope to address – eg, children, students, general adult readers, experts, etc. Investigate the competition – other books on the same subject, at various readership levels. Identify a gap in the market – some way in which you can write your book so that it will differ from its competitors. Identify the publishers most likely to be interested in your book: most publishers have (fairly) clear areas of interest.

3 Commence further subject RESEARCH: you will already know a lot about your chosen subject but more research will certainly be needed. This will continue in parallel with all the other work as the book progresses.

4 Prepare a SALES PACKAGE – my own term for the material with which you will seek to interest a publisher. It will consist of a) a detailed synopsis and b) a statement of the book's purpose, its potential market, how it will differ from its competitors and why you are the ideal author.

5 Interest a PUBLISHER in your proposal – through your sales package. Once interest has been aroused, be prepared to discuss and adjust the synopsis (and possibly the target readership) to the publisher's requirements. Be flexible, not dogmatic.

6 Write one or two SAMPLE CHAPTERS – ideally have them almost ready before discussions with the publisher. They should not exceed about twenty per cent of the total book. They must be first class – and complete in every respect.

7 Negotiate and sign an AGREEMENT with the publisher – before you write any more of the book. Watch out particularly for realistic delivery date and total length. Press for an advance against future royalties – but don't be too surprised if you don't get one.

8 WRITE the book. Work to the agreed synopsis, and ideally, to a word budget and timetable.

9 DELIVER the completed book manuscript. This is not the end of the 'writing' work though. You still have to work closely with the publisher on revisions (a chapter may need rewriting or merely rearranging), editing, proof-reading, finalising the index, etc.

10 Help the publisher to SELL the book.

As you can see, there is more to writing a non-fiction book than just writing it. It's a lot of work. The successful non-fiction author is the person who meets all the above professional requirements. And the steps to successful publication are markedly different from those which need to be followed by the aspiring novelist.

As illustrated in the above 'ten steps' – and reverting to the comparison, at the start of this chapter, between writing fiction and non-fiction – the non-fiction author has one important advantage over the novelist.

The non-fiction author nearly always gets a publisher's firm commitment to the proposed book before much of it is written. It is customary for a publisher to sign an Agreement with a non-fiction author – even a first-time author – on the basis of a synopsis plus sample chapters. And most Agreements provide for a partial advance against royalties on signature. In other words, the non-fiction author gets some money 'up front'. (More details on Agreements, royalties, advances, etc. are in Chapter 10.)

Write to sell

To retain your enthusiasm to keep going, while at the same time subjecting yourself to all the work and the trauma of getting your book into the shops, you need a good reason for writing it. (That is – before you sign the Agreement and are paid an advance.)

What then is your reason? Money? You could well do better cleaning windows or stacking supermarket shelves. Status, kudos, recognition? These factors can certainly be an important part of your reason for writing – just as money too can be a part. But neither money nor kudos should be the main reason for writing your book. On their own they are likely to lead to unenthusiastic 'hack' writing.

If you are going to write a book, you must believe that there is a need for it; that you can produce something that others will find useful, interesting and of value. You must enjoy the writing too, the organising, the careful stringing together of the words. You can't not write your book.

Your conviction that there is a need for your book, and your personal need to write it must be accompanied by the supporting prospect of money and kudos. Altogether, they amount to a believable reason for writing it. (Beware, though, a conceited or over-inflated view of your own ability.)

But all these reasons for writing must be subjugated to the requirements of the marketplace. If your book is not written with the customer in mind . . . it won't sell. It will not be a saleable proposition in the bookshops and you will find it impossible to sell the concept to a publisher. If the publisher thinks it won't sell, he won't buy. You'll have wasted your time and effort writing it.

You must write what the customer wants. All the time you are writing your non-fiction book you must think of the needs of the reader – which means that first you have to identify your reader.

The world of publishing

First-time writers of non-fiction sometimes find the thought of adjusting what they want to write to fit the needs of the reader – as represented by the publisher – irksome. But it is no use writing a book just for yourself; unless there are readers, you are not communicating.

The plus side of the coin is that, if there is a need (and 'room') for your book and if it's any good, you will find someone to publish it for you. There are hundreds of publishers – many with several imprints – in Britain alone; without new books to publish they will go out of business. Publishers need new books – to produce those tens of thousands of new titles each year. But they're in business: they have to make a profit to survive. They will exercise their best judgement to ensure that they only take on commercially viable propositions.

Major publishers need books that will sell nationally and, even better, internationally. There are also many smaller, locally based or specialist publishers who will consider books of local or specialist interest. To repeat, if there is a viable – ie. profitable – market for your book, and if it's any good, someone will publish it for you.

Let me clarify. The phrase 'will publish it for you' means the author supplying the text (and illustrations as appropriate) and the publisher – entirely at his own expense – converting the pages of typescript into printed books and marketing them. The publisher pays the author: usually a percentage of the sales figures, sometimes a lump sum payment. The author does not pay the publisher.

(Very occasionally, a reputable publisher will seek to negotiate sponsorship – a subsidy – for a book. The book could, for example, be the history of a large organisation which might agree to pay part of the cost of publication in order to hold down the sale price. Or the organisation might contract to take a number of copies for distribution to members or customers. Even more seldom, a wealthy author might perhaps subsidise the quality of the book's production. Such subsidies however almost always come after – and do not influence – the 'literary' acceptability of the book.)

It was necessary to explain the normal world of publishing in order to comment on the alternatives: self-publishing and so-called 'vanity publishing'.

Self-publishing

Self-publishing is – occasionally – a practical alternative to conventional publishing. It is often the only course of action for authors of books of extremely narrow specialism or local interest. It may be the right thing for a village history or a 'How To' book about a small-interest hobby or craft. It is often the only way for a poet – outside the scope of this book – to achieve publication.

Self-publishing should never be the automatic recourse of an author seeking to avoid the editorial changes asked for by a commercially minded conventional publisher. Changes for commercial reasons are often worth making; at least, never reject them without serious consideration. Self-publishing ought to be market-oriented too.

But let me define self-publishing. The self-publishing author:

● writes a book
● decides that it warrants publication
● finances the entire publication of the book
● edits it (or pays a professional editor to edit it)

- designs and typesets the page layout (or pays a professional book designer to prepare the edited text for typesetting and printing)
- negotiates with a printer for the production of a number of copies of the book to be printed (the print-run being determined, hopefully on realistic commercial grounds, by the author), and
- arranges for all that goes into the marketing of the book (publicity, selling to individual bookshops, etc.)

All of the above is possible and, where the author knows well the market for the book – the villagers and the few local bookshops, or the specialist craft, etc. magazines and organisations – practical too. But the activity is much more than just the writing. It entails the investment of much of the author's time – and money.

The ready availability of the personal computer (PC) has made self-publishing a more viable proposition. So-called Desk-top Publishing (DTP) programs – which, in fact, do no more than the equivalent of typesetting and page layout – put more of the publishing process within reach of the author. But again, it all takes time.

Without doubt, self-publishing is a viable proposition for any author of a narrow-interest, ultra-specialist non-fiction book. But don't go into it without your eyes wide open: it's a lot of non-writing work and can eat up capital. Try to find a 'proper' publisher first, before going down the self-publishing road.

Vanity publishing

Vanity publishing is different – and to be avoided at all costs. It gets its name from the way in which virtually every manuscript offered to the 'publisher' is deemed worthy of acceptance and publication.

Vanity publishers are not hard to identify. They advertise for writers with a book 'that merits publication' or suchlike. They sometimes tell you, in their advertisements, that they are 'shared-cost' or 'joint-venture' publishers. Whatever they may tell you, your 'share' of the – usually excessive – costs will be far from equal . . . and certainly not fair. Vanity publishers' profit comes entirely from your 'contribution'. Once you are 'hooked', they have no risk, their profit is secure, and they offer no commitment to your book.

No reputable publisher needs to advertise for books; they are usually swamped with unsolicited manuscripts – mostly unsuitable. A real publisher stakes – ie. risks – his money and his professional reputation on each book that he publishes under his imprint. He is – rightly – 'choosy'.

Vanity publishers seldom produce more than a small number of bound copies of their books. They may print more sheet-copies – the 'publishers' are often little more than jobbing printers and print run-ons are not costly – but these are seldom bound.

Vanity publishers are well known to booksellers; their books are seldom if ever found on bookshop shelves. This is another way of identifying vanity publishers: check the shelves of libraries and bookshops; their books are almost never to be found.

Vanity publishers are singularly unselective in what they accept for publication; one poet has documented how he deliberately offered more than one copy of some poems in a poor-quality batch for publication – this duplication was not even noticed when they were 'accepted'. They'll praise and publish anything – you're paying. You're calling the tune.

If any 'publisher' advertises for authors, and then seeks a financial contribution towards the cost of publication as a condition of acceptance . . . run for cover. This is shark-infested territory.

The variety of non-fiction books

But enough of the various types of publisher. Henceforth this book deals with the relationship of author and conventional publisher. Much of the advice is equally relevant to the author contemplating self-publishing. Let us now review the wide variety of types of non-fiction book that are published.

We can classify non-fiction books under two broad headings: those that are basically 'TECHNICAL' and those that are basically 'STORYLINE'. There are, as we shall explain later, fundamental differences in the way these two non-fiction categories should be handled. Let me first, though, explain and define the two general handled. Let me first, though, explain and define the two general categories.

I classify as basically 'technical' non-fiction books:

● all textbooks (irrespective of subject, from the 'purest' art to the 'purest' science via technology of all kinds, and irrespective of target readership level, from pre-school toddler to post-graduate professor)
● all 'How To' books (again, being textbooks in all but name, irrespective of subject – craft, hobby, sport, pastime, work-skill, etc. – and target readership)
● all 'collecting' books (giving information, for all levels of readership, about types of animal, vegetable or mineral collectables – including birds' eggs, fishes or sea-shells, plants, porcelain figurines, church windows or brass rubbings, statues, pop records, garden gnomes . . . and even the requirements of publishers and magazine editors. 'Collecting' books often have some overlap with 'How To' books too – eg. cookbooks)

Under the broad heading of 'storyline' non-fiction books, I would include:

● biographies and autobiographies of all types – from the brief, personal-experience account of an 'ordinary person's' unusual or amusing week/month/year, to the heavyweight biography of a major historical or political character – for all readership levels, toddler to professor
● all histories – eg. of a five-day war, of the struggle for control of a commercial company, of a sports club or organisation, of a specific World Cup (any sport) competition or Tour de France race . . . or even the story of the universe from start to present-day – again, all readership levels
● books about social policies – such as the thoughts of a leading politician
● books about travel – experiences, as opposed to guide-books, which I would classify within the 'technical' category. And I would group the glossy British Heritage type of picture-book within this sub-category – being 'travel at home'

And I think – purely because they would probably be treated in a similar fashion – I would also include here, the odd-one-out . . .

● books of humour

Inevitably my non-fiction categorisation is a broad-brush, subjective approach. You may wonder where a particular book of yours fits into this scheme of things. Don't worry. There are differences in the way you move your book forward – mostly at the synopsis stage – which are explained as this book proceeds. But these differences are mainly in the way you approach the publishers; they are thus of initial importance only. No publisher is going to reject a book because your approach is slightly unusual; if the idea is good, the publisher will ask for anything he thinks is missing.

And, for the avoidance of doubt and confusion throughout the rest of this book: I shall refer to publishers as male and editors as female – which is often correct. But, of course, the terms and comments are equally appropriate to female publishers and male editors. I'm not sexist – just a lazy writer. (I've tried to refer to authors as either male or female – which too is correct.) Now, with that disclaimer out of the way – the basic idea.

1

THE BASIC IDEA

The fact that you are reading this book suggests that you have already decided to write a non-fiction book. Before we look in detail at how you should proceed, let's think a little more about the types of non-fiction book.

Too many aspiring authors' first thoughts are to write about . . . themselves. They think that this will be an easy non-fiction book to write. It will not be; it can be one of the most difficult.

Because they themselves like reading biographies and autobiographies, they assume that others will be similarly interested in the story of their own eventful lives. Again, they are probably wrong.

Think again about the autobiographies that you have enjoyed reading, the ones that perhaps became best-sellers. It is likely that they were the lives of well-known, if not famous, people. Biographies of the unknown must tell of really spectacular experiences – which will, themselves, generate at least short-term fame.

Are you already famous or are your experiences sufficiently unusual, newsworthy, or funny to generate the necessary 'fifteen minutes' of fame? Unless you can put your hand on your heart and answer yes to one or other of those alternatives – or are writing solely for your own family's consumption . . .

DON'T WRITE YOUR MEMOIRS.

The only other 'justification' for writing about yourself is when you believe – and can persuade a publisher – that others can *learn* from your experiences. (Excellent examples of such light autobiographies are those published by the religious presses. They are written by 'ordinary' people recounting their personally important, but seldom world-shattering, religious experiences. They serve a purpose: to encourage others down a similar path.)

Biographies (or 'ghosted' autobiographies) of well-known personalities are certainly a possibility. The 'ordinary' writer, though, should usually avoid the 'heavyweight' historical biography; academic writers will jealously guard their inside track on such books. There is *some* scope for established writers to 'ghost' the biographies of others, but this is no job for anyone without a 'track record'. Similarly, to write an entertainment world biography it's almost essential to have 'inside' contacts.

Generally, there are more opportunities for a non-fiction book in the broadly defined 'technical' area. Whether 'technical' or 'story-line', though, you must define the subject.

A book about what?

Now that I have persuaded you not to write your memoirs, what *are* you going to write about?

Some people know a lot about their job or hobby, or some facet of it; some are enthusiastic about an outdoor sport or an indoor game; some are interested in specialist areas of the arts or have experience of some aspect of health-care; some collect artefacts, others collect factual information. Many people have some knowledge and/or experience that can be shared with others. Identify *your* subject.

Take a sheet of paper; write down – in as few words as possible – the subject you propose to write about. Now think more about this subject. If you are to write a book about something, you must really know the subject well.

(There is no better way of ensuring that you know a subject well than by having to write about it. All those minor aspects that you glossed over in your mind must now be explained in detail. This is when you discover, to your horror, that you didn't really understand it after all. In compensation, though, once you have 'mugged up' those missing bits, in order to write about them, you will be that much more knowledgeable yourself.)

Break the subject down into sub-topics. These can be periods in a person's life, stages in a process, aspects of a game (eg. training, rules, tactics, etc.), alternative ways of achieving an end, and so on. Do you know enough about each of these sub-topics to write about them in depth? Have you just divided the subject into those aspects of which you are well aware, or is it really a comprehensive coverage of the subject? Are you thinking about the whole subject ... or just the part that interests you?

It is not necessarily wrong to restrict a subject to those parts that interest you. What is important is that the restricted subject can stand alone in its own right.

Let me illustrate that point. A broad, general-interest book about practical gardening could quite reasonably omit any reference to the science of soil chemistry. The ordinary gardener doesn't need to know. It would not be acceptable, though, to exclude all mention of planting timetables or fertiliser requirements.

But the whole subject of practical gardening could be narrowed down. Without being a gardener myself, I can envisage books on eg. the small city garden, gardening for those with little time (*The Hour-a-Week Gardener* sounds good to me), or growing delphiniums. Such refining of a subject is perfectly acceptable; indeed, it is often the best way of finding a suitable book-subject.

But don't narrow your subject down too far. It must be sufficient to warrant a book about it.

Demand and scope

It is not enough, though, merely to consider whether a subject is big enough to write about. Is the subject one that people will want to buy a book about? How many people? You may be the world's leading expert on double-ended oojimaflips and have much to write about them – but is anyone else in the world interested in them?

Even the most specialist of publishers will hope to sell a couple of thousand copies of any book he publishes, and many of these sales could be to libraries, which implies multiple readership. You need to think of a subject that will appeal to at least several thousand people. And the broader the scope of the book, the larger the potential readership.

If your basic idea is too small or too narrow a specialism to warrant a book in its own right or attract sufficient readership, broaden its scope.

If you yourself are not capable of broadening the scope, consider collaboration with another writer. It is sometimes possible to write a book with another specialist, equally as narrow as yourself perhaps, and produce a worthwhile, saleable joint effort. (You would be well advised, though, to agree in advance on your individual responsibilities and the apportionment of the royalties. I recommend an exchange of formal letters recording the Agreement. For more on royalties, *see* chapter 10.)

If there is only a relatively small – but important – aspect of your chosen subject on which you are not competent to write, you might negotiate with a colleague to write a specific chapter on that aspect for you. (You should reserve the right to edit your colleague's text – subject to post-edit check – to ensure that it conforms to the style of the rest of the book, which is yours. And it is best to compensate a one-chapter collaborator with a lump sum payment rather than a share of future royalties.)

Extending collaboration somewhat further, there is also the possibility of a compiled handbook – several individual chapters, each written by a specialist in his own field – the whole book being organised and pulled together by an editor. (This concept is further examined in Chapters 4 and 6.)

Another important factor affecting the demand for the book and influencing the scope and coverage, is the educational level at which the book is pitched. The aspiring non-fiction author must all the time consider the needs of the reader. The coverage and treatment will differ widely if the potential reader is a scientist or a schoolchild. (My own knowledge of computer technology is strictly limited. I could never write an adult book about computers. Yet, many years ago when primary schoolchildren were less computer-aware than they are now, I was able to write a simple – and successful – children's book, explaining what a computer was and what it does: *What is a Computer?* Blackie, 1970.)

The competition – other people's books

At this early stage in the non-fiction authorship process, when you are still working on the basic idea for your book, you must investigate the opposition – competing books. Unless you are very lucky – or have chosen a too-unusual subject – there will already be several books on the same subject. You must investigate them all – or as many as possible – before starting to write your own.

If your subject is a specialist one you may think you know all the competing books; you might be wrong. You must check. If your subject is broad and of general interest, check the competition at the same level as you propose.

Consult the in-volume bibliographies of all your own books on your chosen subject. Discount – but note – the long-out-of-date titles. Look for reasonably current competing titles and try to get your hands on them, even if only for a brief skim through.

Visit your local library: consult the listings of books on your subject; browse through the relevant sections of the shelves – glance at all the competing titles, borrow the best; chat to the librarian – not only about available and competing titles, but also about their relative popularity (check the number of recent date-stamps in the front of relevant books too).

Investigate the shelves of your local bookshop; await a slack period and talk to the proprietor – he may know of less directly related titles. While you're there, notice which publishers handle your type of book – and which, in your view, handle them best (striking covers, good binding, advertising posters, etc.) This information will be of use later.

You need to get a *feel* for the whole of the opposition: the level at which they are pitched, the breadth and depth of their coverage, their treatment, and whether, in your view, the books are good value for money. If you owned all of the competing books, would you still buy another ... specifically the one you propose to write?

If yours is to be a 'technical' type book, you must think about how your book can carve out a new slice of what is a relatively fixed market. Your book will have to sell at the expense of someone else's book. Whose? Why? If yours is a 'storyline' type book, how long ago was its closest competitor published? Is it time yet for the next book?

Your book is obviously, in your view, going to be better – in some, perhaps small, way – than the competition. (If not, why are you thinking of writing it?) You need to be able to explain why your book is needed: which vacant niche in the wall of information it will fill.

Maybe your book will explain the subject more simply; maybe it will go into much more detail about one important aspect of the subject. (Perhaps it should therefore concentrate on that aspect alone?) Maybe new information has become available – and best of all, only to you. Maybe all the existing books seem to be written for American readers – and you will be writing for a British readership. Maybe you can identify a group of readers – male, female, teenagers, technicians, etc. – not yet, or not adequately, catered for.

Or, even, you have found a publisher whose ongoing series lacks a book on the subject you propose. Even if the market is full of children's books on eg. dinosaurs, every publisher wants his book on them. For completeness. (I know: I've written one.)

There always seems to be room for another good book on virtually any subject: as long as it is better in some way, or fills a need.

Do not treat lightly, or rush, this survey of competing books. It is important for two reasons. First, it will give you ideas on how – or how not – to treat the subject in your own book. And on the way, you will inevitably pick up snippets of new information – it's all useful research (*see* Chapter 2). Secondly, later in the book-writing process, when you have gained the interest of a publisher, he will want to know about the competition and the ways in which your book will be better. He will need to decide how to direct his sales campaign for your book – and how to convince those who own the competing books to buy yours too.

You can only answer the publisher's queries from detailed knowledge. To win, you must know your enemy.

2

RESEARCH – COLLECTING AND ORGANISING MATERIAL

This book is about writing non-fiction. The dictionary defines non-fiction as 'literary matter based directly on fact'. The most important thing about a non-fiction book is the factual information it conveys. To some extent – particularly in the more academic textbooks – literary style is of less importance and can be corrected, as long as it is clear. The quality of the information is what matters; inaccuracy is a cardinal sin for a non-fiction author.

The need for research

A non-fiction author is therefore, necessarily and above all, someone who collects information about a chosen subject – or subjects. The non-fiction author must know all there is to know in the chosen field – subject always to the level at which the book is to be written. This can mean detailed specialised knowledge of a small aspect of a subject; knowing, for instance, more than anyone else in the world about an esoteric subject such as 'the production of gold amalgams in zero-gravity conditions'. It can also mean knowing more than is ordinarily necessary about all aspects of a broad subject. This would cover, for instance, a secondary school mathematics teacher who knows more than is required, about every part of the current syllabus – but without post-graduate knowledge of any single part.

The non-fiction author needs to collect all sorts of information about the chosen subject – even if that subject is the writer's own life. (Your mother will probably remember more about your childhood days than you can recall yourself. You must tap this research source.

For more advice on various research sources, see below.)

The non-fiction author must be aware of most, if not all, of the books that have been published in the field – and even of any new laws, etc. But books alone are not enough. It is important to be up-to-date, which means regularly collecting material from magazines and newspapers. The collection of material is a long, ongoing process.

It is unusual – and potentially disastrous – to decide on a specialist subject for a non-fiction book . . . and only then, at that stage, to start collecting material.

It is always best to select a book subject from, or 'within reach of', the broad scope of one's existing interests. There will always be a need to collect further specific, more detailed material but this research is best done from a broad foundation of related knowledge. The time-honoured advice, *write about what you know*, is certainly well founded – even though I would extend it to be: *get to know your subject well before writing about it.*

The advice about working within existing areas of interest merits explanation and qualification. It is clearly relevant to an idea for a book about 'gold amalgams . . .' or a mathematics textbook.

But what about a book on, say, 'walking in Wales'? You might think that this would entail no more research than to go walking with your eyes open. I'm sure though that an inveterate non-walker like myself, almost totally uninterested in flora, fauna and archaeology, would be at a marked disadvantage in trying to write such a book. A keen walker, interested in the breeding habits of the 'lesser spotted chaffinch', the birds and bees, and the background to all those piles of old stones, would have a good head start on me. Such an 'outdoor person' would probably have a lot of background knowledge about things Welsh before starting on any actual 'walking research'. They would know what to look out for.

But don't be frightened by this talk of 'research'. The non-fiction author doesn't need to re-invent the wheel or rediscover penicillin. Research, to a writer, means the collection and collating of information. It need not entail – but of course does not preclude – physical or mental discovery. A writer does not have to extend the bounds of all human knowledge – merely the knowledge of the reader. The planned level of readership will also influence the amount – and depth – of necessary research: research for a non-fiction book for primary school children need not be as detailed as that for a degree-level text. When researching a non-fiction book for children at primary-school level, my first port of call is usually the children's section of my local library.

Plagiarism and copyright

The problems of plagiarism and copyright are frequently raised in the context of writers' research – and rightly so. But some aspiring authors worry too much about them; they need not be a major constraint. It was once, flippantly, explained to me that if I consulted just one book before I wrote something, the result probably constituted plagiarism. If I consulted two books, this was legitimate research. This advice was over-simplistic – but it contains a measure of common sense.

There can be no copyright of a fact, nor of an idea. Copyright only applies to the form in which the fact or idea is expressed – that is, the way in which the words are strung together.

It is not enough to quote the source of a quotation from another's work. A credit line does not absolve the 'copying author' of an infringement of copyright. Although any direct quotation is legally an infringement, it is accepted practice that brief quotations may be made for purposes of review or criticism. Brief *attributed* quotations *for purposes other than criticism* or review are also often made without the express permission of the copyright owner – and as long as they are brief, are usually permitted by default. When in doubt though, a non-fiction author should always seek the permission of the copyright owner for any quotation.

Plagiarism is less easy to define. In academic circles a technical paper based on the unacknowledged research of another would certainly be plagiarism; if nothing else, the 'author' would be attracting undeserved kudos. In more everyday writing circles, a close and lengthy paraphrase of another's work might be classified as plagiarism. When in doubt, seek permission – and generally, avoid over-close paraphrasing of others' work. Which brings us back to the flippant introduction to this section: consult a number of research sources, not just one.

Research sources

A non-fiction author cannot survive on book research alone. The non-fiction author must collect information – both ongoing and specific, for a new book – from a variety of sources. These will include:

- personal observation, experience (own and others') and expertise
- original research – questionnaires, interviews and correspondence
- material gleaned from journals, magazines, newspapers, etc.
- books – one's own and those borrowed, eg. from libraries
- odds and ends – ephemera, brochures, radio and TV programmes, etc.

No one source will normally suffice on its own.

Personal observation, experience and expertise are potentially the most valuable research sources available to a non-fiction author. Impossible without involvement, personal experience can lead to committed writing; certainly it ensures detailed knowledge. Experience lets you incorporate personal anecdotes in your writing. This can be extremely valuable.

Both this book and its twin sister, *The Craft of Writing Articles* – and many of my other books – are examples of work based largely on personal experience. I've been there. I've done it. Often.

Over many years of writing articles and non-fiction books, I have tried out several different ways of working. Some were good, some less so. I've tried to read just about every available book on non-fiction writing; from them, I've taken on board anything I thought worthwhile and practical. This book represents a crystallisation of those many years of experience – plus material from other sources.

Questionnaires, interviews and general correspondence are, in many ways, a natural extension of personal experience as a source of material for the author. Such methods, though, are not always appropriate.

I could have despatched a questionnaire to other non-fiction authors, seeking information on how they write their books – their work-style. Their responses about their professional approach – preparation, dealing with publishers, etc. – would almost certainly be fairly similar to my own. The variations would probably relate to such things as their daily output, choice of word processor program, whether or not they use a lap-top or desk-top computer, or their working hours. You would be no better off if I were to tell you that x per cent of non-fiction authors use WordPerfect, y per cent have pop music playing in the background while they're working (as I do), and z per cent never write a word before 7.00 pm. Knowing others' work-style preferences wouldn't make me change mine; I doubt if you would change yours.

When I'm working on the regular biennial editions of my market research books (*The Magazine Writer's Handbook* and *The Book Writer's Handbook*), though, questionnaires come into their own. These books contain masses of regularly updated information; much of it from editors' and publishers' responses to my questionnaires. The readers want to see the responses to the questions – they are of *use*.

Most non-fiction authors keep themselves up-to-date with goings-on in at least that part of their field that interests them. Certainly the successful ones do. Usually this entails reading the appropriate specialist journals. (I read most, if not all, of the writing magazines regularly – and others, of course.) Specialist magazines will carry reviews of most of the new books in your field – so at least you will know what you have not yet read.

It is also important not to neglect small news items relevant to your interests/disciplines – in daily papers, etc. Cut them out, mark the source, stick them on larger sheets of paper (A4 paper is recommended, see below) and file them carefully.

But few of us can afford to buy our own copies of all the magazines relevant to all our interests; many of us have to borrow, or share others' copies. Were it not for the photocopier – often available as coin-operated facilities in public libraries, or in local shops – we would need to make notes of important articles, etc. Photocopies are (relatively) cheap; they should be an important part of every non-fiction author's research 'library'. (Where you can, of course, tear out the relevant magazine pages and file those rather than photocopying.)

A word of advice, based on hard personal experience. Many years ago, I extracted – from a writing magazine – and saved the articles which interested me. I now find that many of the incomplete articles on the backs of the torn-out pages look more interesting than the 'front ones' I originally saved. Save 'research articles' of even the most marginal interest – they'll pay off in years to come.

A successful non-fiction author is squirrel-like, saving more and more snippets of possibly valuable information. Make sure you save it in an organised and retrievable way though. More on storage and retrieval systems later.

And so we come, as research sources, to books. A non-fiction author should, as far as possible, read all the books in his/her field.

(Set aside your prejudices against marking books. Underline important sections and make marginal explanatory notes – in your own books. Marked-up books are more useful – easier to extract information from – than those in pristine condition. Books are for use.) Don't restrict your reading to those books of immediate interest and 'appropriate level', either. Read all around your subject; explore beyond its fringes in order to understand the main subject better.

With books, though, even more than with magazines, few authors can afford to buy their own copies of everything relevant. Some must be borrowed. It is neither financially practicable nor legally permissible to photocopy large chunks of a book – nor is a simple copy or extract what is usually required. Of far more use to the non-fiction author would be a few pages of notes, summarising whole chapters, plus the odd, brief, verbatim extract.

And finally, in this review of research sources: don't forget the often-overlooked 'odds and ends'.

Some aspiring non-fiction authors concentrate on books and magazines and overlook the unconventional. A lot of detailed research goes into the making of radio and television documentaries: the wise non-fiction author records and saves relevant programmes for possible future reference. Publicity brochures and advertisements too will often provide useful background information for non-specialist non-fiction books. It is always worth retaining odd bits of relevant ephemera too – tickets, programmes, etc. – as *aides memoire*, if nothing else. (I even have several beer mats in my files – with snippets of useful information on their reverse sides.)

About books and libraries

Books will usually be borrowed from ... (mostly public) libraries. It helps if one understands a little about how books are classified and how libraries are organised.

All books, published anywhere in the world – fiction and non-fiction alike – now carry a unique ten-digit International Standard Book Number (ISBN). Libraries and booksellers alike base their records (and ordering systems) on the ISBN. A book's ISBN will usually be found on page iv of the *prelims* (the pages at the front of a book, before the text proper – further explanation later); it will usually be repeated – both as number and in electronically readable bar-code form – on the back cover of a paperback or on the jacket of a hardback book.

An understanding of the ISBN system is not an essential for the non-fiction author – but it is useful to know.

The ISBN system, operated in Britain by the Standard Book Numbering Agency Ltd, uses a ten-digit number unique to each book and edition. Every ISBN has four distinct, but variable-sized, sections separated by spaces. The four sections of an ISBN represent, in order:

● the country code (For example, 0 and 1 denote that the publisher is based in an English-speaking country; 2 is French-speaking, and so on. Many countries have multi-digit codes – some of my books are published in [English-speaking] Singapore whose country codes are 9971 and 981.)

● the publisher prefix (Within the 0 and 1 country codes, all publishers have at least 2-digit publisher numbers – which accommodate almost one million titles each; smaller publishers have more digits in their publisher prefix. Thus, for example, Harper Collins has publisher prefixes 00 and 01, McGraw-Hill has 07, Penguin 14, Macmillan 333, and Allison & Busby 74900. A small self-publisher could be allocated a seven-digit publisher prefix.)

● the title identifier (That part of the ISBN which, within the specific publisher's list, is unique to the book; it will have as many digits as necessary to retain, with the check digit, the overall 10-digit consistency.)

● the check digit (A number which, read with the other digits, 'proves' the correctness of the whole ISBN.)

To illustrate, this book has the ISBN: 0 74900 277 8 (*see* page iv), which is translated:

0	74900	277	8
English-speaking country	Allison & Busby	*How To Write Non-Fiction Books*	Check

Similarly, one of my children's novels, published in Singapore, has the ISBN: 9971 0 0330 9, which translates:

9971	0	0330	9
Singapore	EPB Publishers Pte Ltd	*The Dragon Who Sneezed*	Check

ISBNs will be helpful/necessary when you wish to order a book (from bookseller or library) but they will not help you locate a book on the library shelves. For that purpose you need to understand the classification system. Most British libraries have adopted the Dewey Decimal system of book classification.

The Dewey system classifies books under ten main classes, from 000 by hundreds to 900, which can be sub-divided again and again, using as many as six or seven digits, separated if necessary by decimal points.

The main classes and sample sub-divisions are:

000 General works
100 Philosophy
200 Religion
300 Social sciences
400 Languages
500 Pure science
600 Technology .... 610 Medicine
700 Fine arts   620 Engineering .... 621 Mechanical
800 Literature   630 Agriculture   622 Mining

900 History	etc.	623 Military
		624 Civil
		etc.

Subject to the views of the individual librarian, this book is probably classified as Dewey 808, meaning:

8   Literature
80   Rhetoric (composition) and collections
808 Technique of oral and written communication

Biographies are treated differently under Dewey; they are usually shelved separately and arranged alphabetically under the surname of the subject person.

Particularly in America, the US Library of Congress classification system is widely used. It uses a combination of letters and numbers to classify books. This extends the range from Dewey's ten main classes to a potential twenty-six. The main Library of Congress classes are:

A   Encyclopedias and reference books
B   Philosophy, psychology and religion
C   Antiquities and biographies
D   History
E/F American history
G   Geography and anthropology
H   Social sciences, economics, sociology
I   Political science
L   Education
M   Music
N   Fine arts
P   Language and literature
Q   Science
R   Medicine
S   Agriculture and veterinary science
T   Technology
U   Military science
V   Naval science
Z   Books, libraries, bibliographies.

There is usually more than one letter in a Library of Congress classification, followed by three or four numbers and then – in some libraries – by the first three letters of the author's surname. If this book were to be looked for under the Library of Congress system, it would probably be found classified as PN145, which means:

P	N	145
Language and literature	Fine arts	Authorship, general works (theory and techniques)

Note-taking

Nothing, perhaps, is more valuable to an non-fiction author than his or her own personal notes. All writers will gradually develop their own note-taking methods – but a few hints may help the beginner. The sort of notes a writer needs will differ from those that will satisfy a non-writer.

A prime essential in any writer's note is the source. It is recommended that the full title of the book and the author's name be the first things to be noted down. This is both common sense and common courtesy – to be able to cite the source when challenged. But a writer also needs to record the publisher's name and the copyright date and edition.

It is also worth recording – in the heading to one or more pages of notes – details of where the book was borrowed from. If the book was borrowed from or consulted at a library it is helpful to record the ISBN, the Dewey or 'L of C' classification and ... at which library the book is kept. (Some special interest books may not be available from your local library; they can, though, be specially borrowed for you from any library in the country. If you can tell your friendly local librarian where the book was previously borrowed from it should expedite reborrowing.)

If the book was borrowed from a friend or contact, or – as perhaps in the case of a biography – consulted in a family library, it will be helpful to record details. You may need to reconsult. Memory of where a particular book was will always prove fallible at just the wrong time. (And if you are bad at returning borrowed books you will soon have fewer friends.)

Depending on the type of research, the notes themselves might be brief summaries of all chapters, or merely notes of particular points of interest. Sometimes you will wish to quote verbatim; at other times you will merely wish to make an *aide memoire*. (But beware: after several years, most *memoires* need a lot of *aide*ing! Fuller notes usually repay the extra time they take.) It is, of course, essential that all notes are correct and accurate; inaccuracy can be disastrous.

Whatever type of notes you make, always make them on A4 paper (*see* filing advice, below); and leave plenty of space all around them. Cramped notes are almost worthless – in later years they may not even be readable. Blank space on a page not only makes the notes look easier to read, it also provides space for later annotation.

Some note-taking authors alternate blocks of notes down alternate halves of the sheet; this is an excellent idea, but difficult if – like many authors now – you use a portable (lap-top or hand-held electronic notebook) computer for note-taking. For computer notes, it's a good idea to achieve much the same effect by adopting an extra-wide left or right margin – it's the alternating that's difficult. And do print them out – a hard copy is essential. Plenty of 'signpost-headings' and tabulations are also helpful in rereading your notes.

I often find it useful to include the source book-page number. This speeds up relocating a reference – and when you really need to check, time is always short.

With 'technical' subjects, diagrammatic illustrations often provide an effective summary of part of the text. Always photocopy such summary diagrams, even if you're making personal notes from elsewhere in the book. (And remember to record, on the photocopy, its source – including page number and book edition – in case you want to ask permission to reproduce or repeat it.)

Of course, books are not the only source of a non-fiction author's notes. Sometimes – with 'storyline' type books particularly – the non-fiction author will wish to have a record of an interview. Some subjects will not object to the author using a portable cassette recorder: even so, there is merit in transcribing the recording while it is still fresh in your memory. If the subject clams up in front of a recorder, though, the author must rely on making quick – brief –

handwritten notes. These must be written up – and expanded – as soon as possible after the interview.

There will also always be the need for recording (on paper) your personal impressions of all sorts of things – from holiday atmosphere to an interviewee's home and furnishings, from instructional anecdote material to the state of repair of specific historic buildings. The notes themselves should of course be equally as comprehensive – and understandable – as notes from books or other sources.

Storage, filing and retrieval

The research for a book can take a long time. It is a part of the learning process by which you became, or will become, an expert in your field. It would undoubtedly have been helpful if you had been able to read this chapter some while ago. (As in, 'If I were wanting to go *there*, I wouldn't be starting from *here*.') That impossibility apart, let's consider *organisation*.

Your researches will, over time, result in a vast amount of information on paper. This collection of information is fine. A pile of papers in a cardboard box is of little use though; information needs to be organised. The 'ordinary interested reader' may not need to be well organised – the writer does. The non-fiction author must be able to retrieve information when it's needed.

A good first step towards organisation is the simple practice of ensuring that all notes are on A4 pages – double-hole punched for filing. Paste small cuttings onto hole-punched A4 sheets (otherwise, they're easily lost); punch holes in photocopies and pages torn from magazines. File them all. There is nothing sacrosanct about the A4 size but most photocopies, many magazines, and most typing and writing paper are A4, so why not standardise on it?

A good way of storing your A4 sheets safely – and tidily – is to file them all in big lever-arch files. Filing them in this way is safe and tidy – but it's not enough. You need to be able to retrieve all the information you've got on specific aspects of your subject(s) – quickly and easily.

One way of organising the files is to letter each file and number

One way of organising the files is to letter each file and number each sheet therein, as inserted. Each sheet in the file can be listed on 'contents-sheets' at the front of the file. But you still need to find which sheet relates to what aspect of the subject. For that, a separate card-index will help.

Sheet B256 might be a photocopy of an article titled *Dragons in Chinese Art* – dragons being one of my 'things', and a possible future book subject. In the card-index there will already be cards labelled: Dragons – general, Dragons – Chinese, Monsters, Chinese mythology, British folk-lore, etc. On both the 'Dragons – Chinese' and 'Chinese mythology' cards, add a line:

Article, *Dragons in Chinese Art* (*The Lady* 26Jan99) – B256

With the use of such cards it is easy to locate – and extract for easy reference – the relevant article.

This block filing and card-index referencing system is logical, effective and flexible. I commend it to anyone just starting. It is not, though, the system I use. My own system is looser, much less tidy, and ... just grew. As above, it is based on A4 sheets, but the filing system is simpler.

Originally, I used old A4 envelopes – one for each aspect of each subject I am interested in. Nowadays, the tattered envelopes have been replaced with clear plastic folders. Related folders are kept together in card wallet-files which are then stored in a filing cabinet. As a photocopy or page of notes is prepared, it is simply stuffed into the relevant folder. Once a folder becomes too fat, I merely subdivide it.

I can quickly review most of the papers I have on any subject without having to hunt for and retrieve individual documents from within a random store. But my cross-referencing is undoubtedly less than one hundred per cent effective. I would willingly admit that my system is less well organised than the card-index-based one – but I am more interested in writing than in filing. Develop your own filing and retrieval system based on one or other – or neither – of the above methods. But do not, as is all too easy, let the filing become an end in itself. Your objective is to know about your subject in order to write a book – NOT to have the world's best filing system.

3

DEVELOPING THE IDEA

If you are a Booker Prize-winning novelist or have already written several blockbusting best-sellers, then maybe you can just sit back and write. Withdraw from the world, let it pass you by. Publishers can be relied on to come knocking on your door, waving cheque-books.

But the average non-fiction author can't do this. The non-fiction author must be a salesperson; must get out and sell each new book idea. (And no, agents are not always the answer for a non-fiction author; the big money's usually in fiction or 'big-name' non-fiction – and that's where the agents swarm.) To sell, the book itself must be accurately aimed at a market to which, in turn, the publisher can sell.

So far, in our professional approach to non-fiction authorship, all we have done is to think of an idea for a book and to start researching its content. (Depending on the type of book, more or less research will have been completed before contemplating the selling of the idea.) It is still not time to start writing the book. We haven't yet sold it.

The 'sales package'

To sell our book to a publisher we have to have something concrete to sell – what might be called a 'sales package'. We are going to launch a miniature advertising campaign, aimed at publishers, to persuade them to buy our idea for a book. We have to show them that we have thought the idea through and that it has the makings of an attractive book – with good sales potential.

The non-fiction author's sales package should consist of:

- a description of the 'target reader': *who* the book is intended for; who can be expected to need or want to read it
- an assessment of the *market* for the book: the likely size of the market and how the proposed book compares with the competition. Where appropriate, how the book will fit within a publisher's existing series
- the author's *credentials*: why you are the ideal person to write the proposed book – with both knowledge of the subject and the ability to write clearly and convincingly

And, separately:

- a detailed description of what the book will contain: a chapter-by-chapter synopsis – and a good title (which be prepared to change)

The first three items – readership, market and credentials – can sensibly be run together. Think of the run-together items as the first page, the covering proposal introducing the synopsis to follow. Together, the proposal and the synopsis form the sales package – your offer to the publishers.

In many ways, your concept of the target reader is both the paramount prerequisite and the continuing essential of a successful non-fiction book. Unless you really know your readership, you can't give them what they want. And if the potential reader doesn't feel at ease with the way in which the book is written . . . he/she won't buy it.

The target reader

It is in the attitude to the reader that the professional differs most sharply from the amateur writer. The amateur writes what he (or she) wants to read; the amateur writes to please him- or herself. The professional writes what the reader wants. This is not a platitude. The professional writes in language that the reader can understand – without being patronising; the professional explains anything the reader would not know – but not what should be known.

As an example, if I were writing an undergraduate history textbook (for which I am not qualified), I might refer merely to 'the Cade revolt of 1450'. In a more 'popular' non-fiction history book – or for 10-year-olds, perhaps – I would give rather more background and explanation. I'd say something like: 'In 1450 the people of Kent and Sussex rose in revolt against the unscrupulous advisers of pious King Henry VI. They were led by Jack Cade, believed to have been illegitimately related to the House of York.'

To write at just the right level, in just the right tone for the reader, means accurately identifying that reader. Describe your target reader, in writing, in as much detail as possible.

This may entail identifying, for a management text, say, such details as typical job title, functions, responsibilities and age; for a children's textbook – the year and grade at what type of school, perhaps. In other cases the reader may be described merely as a keen walker, interested in 'the birds and the bees' and knowing what to look out for under hedge bottoms. I believe that the age of the typical reader is always important: different age-groups understand different things in different ways – their background knowledge varies.

It is also worth identifying what you think is the reader's prime *need*. In planning this book I identified your need as to know how to structure and communicate your thoughts and the presentation approach most likely to achieve acceptance of your non-fiction book for publication. I can't guarantee you will get it published; I can only tell you how best to go about it. That purpose is in my mind all the while I'm writing the book.

When thinking about and describing your target reader your initial thoughts will usually be of someone of your own nationality. This is understandable but can be too parochial. The English-speaking world includes not only the populations of Britain, the United States of America, Canada, Australia, and New Zealand but also the often English-speaking elite (and others) throughout the third world. When you think globally you have a vastly larger potential market for your book. (But of course, not all books can be targeted at a global market; a guide-book to South of England pubs won't sell many copies in Quebec or Singapore – nor in Liverpool or Glasgow, either.)

For your book to sell in the overseas market, you must bear in mind the needs of the overseas reader. Ask yourself whether the book you are proposing is likely to be of interest to Asian or African readers.

One of my early books was an elementary one, for technicians, called *Traffic Engineering – an Introduction*. The publisher and I decided that overseas readers would probably be interested in such a book. (We were right – about forty per cent of its sales were outside the United Kingdom.)

Having decided that *Traffic Engineering* had overseas sales potential, I had to write it in that knowledge. For example, I included an explanation of the operation of parking meters with the introductory phrase, 'Meters, for those fortunate people who are unfamiliar with them, are . . .'. Purely for British readers, such an explanation would probably have been unnecessary – but even for British readers, the book was better for its inclusion.

The target reader – child or adult; generalist or specialist; British through and through, or x per cent Asian, y per cent African, z per cent American, and only the balance British – must always be uppermost in the non-fiction author's mind. The author must repeatedly consider whether the overseas reader will understand each explanation, side-reference, or description. If not, the passage must be rewritten. Lack of clarity is, for a non-fiction author, a cardinal sin.

One way of coping with the problems of differing levels of understanding is to add either basic explanation or more complicated material 'off line'. This can be in illustrations, appendices or what article-writers call 'side-bars'. (A side-bar is a self-contained, boxed-in supplement to a feature article otherwise complete in itself.) Look at present-day children's encyclopedias, etc., for the effective use of boxed-in 'bites' of extra information. Check with your publisher before adopting this approach though – it is not appropriate in all types of book.

Don't add such extra explanation in the form of footnotes. Footnotes make the typesetter's life more difficult – which means the price goes up – and they look unattractive. They will put off all but the academic reader too.

Think 'book'

Although, above, we mentioned the market assessment and author's credentials before the synopsis – because the overall proposal will most probably be read in that order – the synopsis, like the determination of the target reader, is one of the initial 'building blocks'. It is best therefore to look next at the synopsis.

First, the non-fiction author must *THINK BOOK*.

What is a book? Basically, a book is *book-sized*. (Many in the publishing and bookselling business believe that the public select books largely by weight; undoubtedly a book has to look and feel book-sized if it is to sell.) Thirty thousand words would be on the short side for a book – it's almost a pamphlet or booklet; it is difficult to make it look worth buying. There is virtually no maximum limit; but the longer a non-fiction book is, the more expensive to produce, therefore the higher the list price – and the harder to sell.

To give ourselves something to hold onto, let's think about a non-fiction book containing about forty thousand words – the lower end of the target length for this book. (There's nothing rigid about that figure; I just need it as a basis for what follows.)

Such a non-fiction book might well be divided into eight to twelve chapters, averaging about four to five thousand words per chapter – a good length. (There is nothing really 'wrong' with twenty chapters, each of 2,000 words – but longer chapters are better. A 4,000-word chapter will take up about ten book pages; shorter chapters seldom look big enough. Extra-short chapters suggest that the author doesn't know much about those aspects of the subject. Conversely, a small number of extra-long chapters make a book look difficult – and it's certainly hard to find one's way around in such books.)

The synopsis has to show, in detail, chapter by chapter, the content of your book. And it must do so in a logical, understandable way. Without doubt, preparing the synopsis is one of the most important parts of the process of writing a non-fiction book.

I have, in the Introduction, explained how non-fiction books can all be classified – at least for purposes of the method of approach to publishers – as either 'technical' or 'storyline'. The form in which the synopsis is prepared will vary between the two book types.

Form apart, the synopsis is an essential part of any sales package. We'll look first at the synopsis for the 'technical' book.

The 'technical' synopsis

Set down on a sheet of paper – or maybe on the computer screen, but I still find it easier to do my initial planning-thinking on a sheet of paper – all the separate parts of your subject. At this stage, don't worry about logic or sequence; concentrate on dividing the whole into self-contained parts – and on ensuring that you really have covered it all. Every subject can be sub-divided; if you have not already done so, in your mind at least, now is the time to do it.

My initial thoughts about this book – effectively my 'doodles' – were, in random order:

● attitude of mind – professionalism (the fundamental ethos – don't write until the idea is sold)
● the basic idea – who will read it? (the target reader)
● selling the idea – approaching publishers (don't give up: there are lots of publishers)
● production and publicity – help the publisher to sell your book
● business matters – royalties, Agreements, tax
● organising the content, the structure, and the writing
● writing equipment
● the writing process – write to budget: accuracy, brevity, clarity
● illustrations
● preparing the typescript
● preparing the index – when and how
● editing – difference between commissioning and copy-editors – watch that copy-editor doesn't destroy the sense
● proofs and proof-reading – costs, symbols
● next book – and/or revised edition(s)
● writer's library
● research techniques

That's too many self-contained parts. I don't want more than about ten parts – to make ten chapters. Perhaps some can be rethought and run together?

The next stages – and they tend to run together – are to rearrange the chapter-ideas into a logical sequence and to expand on the contents of each chapter. There is seldom just one single correct sequence – merely different people's opinions. (Some might use a sequence based on: content – writing – selling. I believe that, as in real life, advice on selling should come earlier; my preferred sequence is more like: idea – content – selling – writing. There is – maybe – room for both approaches.) What is important, though, is to ensure that, in order to understand one chapter, the reader is not required to have read a later one. This is not as easy as it sounds, for many techniques need a circular, iterative process.

I made several changes to my initial thoughts.

I wanted to expound my overall 'ten steps' professional approach early on in the book; I also needed to explain how I have grouped the many types of non-fiction book into just two broad types. The answer was an introduction – an addition to my 'basic' ten chapters, which concept I have otherwise stuck to. And an introduction is often a good idea – to indicate how the book will deal with the subject. There was no question that I had to bring research right forward – that was clearly in altogether the wrong place. Business matters too was in too early – and several other 'bits' could indeed, with advantage, be run together. But we needn't labour the rearrangements: compare the initial list with the Contents page. I think the end result makes good sense.

Having decided on the chapters and their sequence, you need to think about what individual chapters will contain. Effectively the same process as before – within a more limited scope. You know what you meant by your initial headings – now expand on them. These 'chapter-expansions' should be fairly brief, yet describe the content adequately.

To illustrate the coverage of a synopsis, the details given for this chapter were:

Developing the idea: The components of the essential sales package to offer to publishers. Define the target reader: explain different treatments for different readers – and need to 'think global'. Need to 'think book' too – say ten chapters, each 4,000 words with explanation of why. The synopsis for the 'technical' book. The 'storyline' book synopsis. How to think of 'selling' titles. Putting the pieces together in the formal proposal (the assessment and credentials part of the sales package) – with example.

When you have thought through each of your chapters and can write something like that for each, you can prepare the overall synopsis.

(You may notice that this chapter does not exactly follow the synopsis details: its 'organisation' was refined during the actual writing process – *see* Chapter 5.)

You may feel that there are some aspects of your subject that don't justify a chapter to themselves. In 'technical' books, one practical solution is to include, at the end, a 'miscellany' chapter – a rag-bag of small, important, but unrelated matters. Another method, of course, is to 'bend' your chapter-subjects to accommodate a section on a related matter. Or you can add an appendix at the end of the book – as I have done with my short list of recommended books.

The purpose of the synopsis is threefold:

1 To demonstrate to the publisher that you intend to cover the subject adequately. (He may wish to suggest further aspects to be covered, which can be helpful to the author.)
2 To act as the first check-list of material to be covered by the author when actually writing.
3 To give a general 'feel' of the proposed book's contents – for the publisher's sales team and, through them, for potential customers.

A warning though. Do not become too firmly committed to your synopsis – for two reasons. First, the publisher who accepts your sales package may wish to vary its content or sequence. Unless you have strong reasons for not complying, it is usually wise to go along with such suggestions; they will be intended to improve the book and its sales potential – and anyway, the publisher is the paymaster, or will be. (Unbending *prima donnas* often have to sing for their supper, rather than being wined and dined . . .)

The second reason for synopsis-flexibility is that, as the book develops, you will find that you wish to make changes yourself. You may find some new or essential aspect that both you and your publisher have overlooked. You must take this on board – absorb it into your synopsis-plan. Remember to keep the publisher 'in the picture' though. Don't surprise him on delivery. (Delivering triplets would be traumatic . . . if twins were expected.)

At the end of your synopsis, say roughly how long – in round thousands of words – you expect the book to be, and whether, and to what extent, it will be illustrated. (*See* also Chapter 7.)

The 'storyline' synopsis

The synopsis for a 'storyline' type of non-fiction book needs a rather different treatment. And I so christened this category of non-fiction book because that is what many of them are: stories – true stories. They can often be approached – synopsis and sales approach – in much the same way as for a novel.

If you are proposing to write a biography, one way of starting the book is with what fiction-writers call a *hook*: something really gripping that will immediately interest the potential reader; some turning point in the career of the subject-person. (I recall the film *Cromwell*. That didn't start at his birth; it dived straight into the story.) This is an approach well fitted to the light, popular type of biography – the type, one might say, most akin to fiction. It is particularly suited to the light autobiography, recording only a small part of the author's whole life-span. The more serious, 'heavier' biographies all tend to be written in full chronological sequence. Antonia Fraser's marvellous *Cromwell: Our Chief of Men* begins, 'In the spring and on the eve of the seventeenth century, a son was born to Robert and Elizabeth Cromwell of Huntingdon. The child was named Oliver; the date was . . .' The book ends with his death.

The synopsis for a 'storyline' type of non-fiction book must show whether the sequence is to be chronological or whether it will include some flashbacks. (Like the hook, the flashback is another fictional technique whereby early 'back-story' is introduced out of sequence to explain some action or attitude.)

The 'storyline' non-fiction author – just like the 'technical' author
– has to think all around the subject. It pays, once again, to list all
the aspects of the subject – the subject-person's life (or that portion
to be covered), the battle or complete war, the sporting occasion, the
country (or the author's own travels) – and then ponder on first their
completeness, and then the 'best' chapter-order in which to include
them. Should you start with the reasons for the war, the history of
the race, the statistics of the country – or should you start with a
bang?

And, unless your book is to be of mainly academic interest, there
is always a good case to be made for starting with something really
interesting. The first page of your book may be all that an
uncommitted bookshop-browser – or publisher's reader – will read;
if it looks boring, there will be no sale.

Even within a chronological chapter-sequence – for biography,
event-story or travel-progress – there will often also be a need for
'offline' chapters.

I have long toyed with the idea of a serious biography of Sylvia
Pankhurst. She was a leading suffragette; but she was much more.
She was an accomplished artist, a poet, a journalist and non-fiction
author and an ardent, before-her-time feminist. She was also an
early British communist – and an Ethiopian 'saint'. My chapter-plan
for this book runs chronologically but with 'offline' chapters on her
writing and other aspects of a fascinating life.

When writing the in-chapter details for a 'storyline' type of non-
fiction book, there needs to be just as much description as for the
'technical' book. You need to demonstrate to the potential publisher
that you intend to cover the subject sufficiently.

Without wishing to suggest that I am an expert in the biography
field, an extract from my draft Sylvia Pankhurst synopsis may be a
useful illustration.

7 Sylvia's War (1914-1918): The family turns 'jingo', while
Sylvia is pacifist and increasingly socialist. She works hard for
'her' East Enders, opening the 'Penny Carltons', the 'Mother's
Arms' (an ex-pub), the toy factory, etc. The League of Rights and
her sweated labour campaign. Her enthusiasm at the Russian
Revolution; she opens/founds the People's Russian Information

Bureau. Her Derby speech. The limited impact of the granting of women's suffrage on Sylvia. The 'coupon' election of 1918.

As for the 'technical' type of non-fiction book, the same warning. Don't get too committed to your synopsis at this stage. Publishers may want to suggest a different coverage or even a different treatment. Be prepared to be as flexible as possible.

There is often more scope, in the 'storyline' type of non-fiction book, for extra material to be included at the end of the book. For my Sylvia book, I envisage a calendar of important events in her life and a list of her many publications as two appendices. If the book were, for example, about the latest Tour de France cycle race, it could usefully have an appendix listing past winners of the race. In a travel book, detailed national statistics would probably fit best in an appendix; a list of important posts held by the author – effectively a CV – would be useful appendix material in a book of political memoirs.

As with the 'technical' book synopsis, end with an estimate of the book's planned length and say whether illustrations are proposed.

Illustrations are frequently appropriate in both 'technical' and 'storyline' types of non-fiction book. The wise author thinks about illustrations all the while the book is being planned and written. There are details about the use of illustrations, and what the author should do about their acquisition and/or preparation in Chapter 7.

The book's title

Another important part of the sales package is a striking title. The title is the author's equivalent of the star-burst-surrounded phrase that attracts the shoppers – 'Special Discount Offer' or 'Beat the Budget – Buy Now'. And like the supermarket sales pitch, it is most effective if it is brief and catchy.

I have found that ideas for a title most often come to me while I am developing the synopsis. At this stage in the process my thoughts are about the *whole* book; when I get down to writing it, I am usually concentrating on on a single aspect – and can't see the wood for ...

The purpose of a book title is to attract favourable attention, to identify the book and, persuasively, to describe its content. And today, it must be brief.

A title such as 'A Manual of Conceptual Design Standards and Policies for Widget Technicians', which might – if it were not a product of my imagination – have been acceptable a hundred years ago, would not be so today. Not only does it look old-fashioned; it is too lengthy to be easily referred to, or to have any sales impact at all, and – of considerable technical/production importance – it would not fit in, as a running head across the pages. The printer would also find it troublesome to print all that on the spine of the book – which, at forty thousand words, is relatively slim.

Subtitles can supplement a short title but they too are no longer favoured, unless they are the only way of adequately describing the book. (One of my textbooks was originally called *Highway Planning Techniques*, which I thought sufficiently clear, but the publisher subtitled it *The Balance of Cost and Benefit*.)

You should never be surprised if your publisher – once you and he are committed – wants to change the title of your book. They often know, better than the author, what makes a good selling title. Go along with their suggestions unless they are really unacceptable. But work at developing a good title yourself, anyway. Even if later discarded, it will have played its part in selling the idea to the publisher.

Aim at a title of no more than four or five main, or key words. In most of my books I have so far succeeded in keeping to that target, while clearly defining the subject of each book. And if you cannot define, concisely, what your book is about, perhaps the subject itself is less self-contained than you thought?

To start you thinking of suitable titles, ask yourself:

● *What will the ('technical') book help the reader to do?* Hence: 'How to Widget', 'Profit from Your Widget', or 'Widgeting for Beginners'.
● *Who or what, specifically, is the book about?* Hence 'Cromwell', 'The Nine-day War', or 'Journeys on a . . . Rhinoceros'.
● *What is the conventional title of the subject?* Can you call your book 'Widgetry Simplified', 'Simple Widgetry', or better, 'Successful Widgetry'?
● *How do you think of yourself?* This might lead to a title such as

'The Successful Widgeter' – or even 'The Compleat Widget'.

Notice the use, in 'technical' type book-titles, of such descriptive, yet persuasive, phrases as 'How To . . .', 'Successful . . .', and 'Profit from . . .'. In each case they suggest that buying your book will enable the reader to do something previously impossible, to succeed, to make money, or to start on a new occupation or hobby.

Notice also that, still in 'technical' non-fiction books, the title clearly indicates the subject. There is no room in this type of non-fiction book for the erudite allusion or partial quotation.

The allusive title is sometimes acceptable for the 'storyline' type of non-fiction book – most often where the author is already a recognis-able 'name'. (I dream of writing a book on beer and brewing entitled 'The Precious Half', alluding to the delightful line in Fitzgerald's *Rubaiyat of Omar Khayam*, 'I often wonder what the Vintners buy/ One half so precious as the Goods they sell' – which I only know so well because it's inscribed on the wall of a favourite hostelry. But this is pure Dreamland; it wouldn't really be a good title.)

The proposal

The other part of the sales package – the proposal – has the role of conveying to the publisher much of the thinking already discussed in this chapter. It is a 'hard sell' document, seeking to persuade the publisher to accept your idea and the accompanying synopsis.

I believe that, ideally, the proposal should be no more than a single – Churchillian – sheet of single-spaced typescript. (The accompanying synopsis should similarly, I believe, be complete within no more than about two sheets of single-spaced typescript, or the equivalent. One school of thought, to which I do not subscribe, recommends double-spaced typing for the proposal and synopsis.)

The proposal needs to show, first:

● Who will buy the proposed book – that is, the target reader

Then, either:

42

- What the book will help the reader to do – or do better
- Why the target reader needs instruction in the book's subject
- Which work position the book will help the reader to approach or aspire to (eg. 'become a managing director' or 'become a foreman widgeter') – OR – Which examination syllabus is relevant to this subject and how thoroughly does the book cover the syllabus?

or:

- What is so special/interesting/unusual/amusing about the ('storyline' type) book subject that will make it an attractive purchase to ordinary readers? (This is the time to 'refresh' the publisher's memory about the amazing characteristics of the subject-person, the spectacular nature of the sport, the attractions of the country – to 'sell' the subject.)
- What anniversary, event or date is forthcoming to which the book's launch can be linked? This launch-date must be far enough ahead to allow time for the book to be considered, commissioned, written, produced and launched – say three years.

Then, equally important for both types of non-fiction book:

- Why you are ideally qualified to write this book – your 'author's credentials'. This is no time for false modesty – sell yourself. (But be careful; once sold, you must live up to your sales line.)
- What competitive books are on the market, how yours will differ and in what ways it is better – and, ideally, the market niche into which you believe your book will fit.
- Roughly how long you expect the book will take to write and deliver.

And here too, as well as at the end of the synopsis (either type):

- Roughly how long you expect the book to be – mentioning your willingness to adjust the length if required – and whether illustrations are planned.

Much of the work that you put into writing this proposal will also

HOW TO WRITE NON-FICTION BOOKS   Proposal   Gordon Wells

In 1993, 60,000 totally new books were published in Britain. Non-fiction books outnumber novels by about six to one; many are by first-time writers.

So, what does it take to become a non-fiction author? Other than the essential ability to *organise* one's thoughts, basically *expertise*. Expertise in *doing* almost anything, from cookery to pet-care, from golf to gardening, from writing to walking in Wales. But it needn't be about a craft- or sport-skill, it can be expertise about a specialist interest - in anything from Meissen china to Welsh love-spoons. There are many opportunities, too, for teachers and professors to write text-books. And there are opportunities for biographies and really interesting autobiographies.

This book is aimed at the potential author of any non-fiction book. It explains, in detail, how to go about it. The craft of writing a non-fiction book is very different from the skill required to write a novel. This book is not for the aspiring novelist.

This book will not guarantee that the reader will produce a best-seller. There may be no market for a book on an esoteric subject, no matter how dear it may be to the writer's heart. But if a writer follows the advice contained in this book, his/her own book will be well structured and professionally presented with the minimum of wasted effort. The book's content, of course, remains the author's responsiblity. There are many opportunities for a non-fiction author. There are few books explaining how to go about it.

There are only two such books currently published in the UK: Neither book is as comprehensive as mine; neither author has anywhere near as much experience in writing non-fiction books as I do. [Another book], while excellent, deals with all types of book, not just non-fiction, and in a somewhat diverse fashion. There are American books on the subject - but US practices are not readily transferable to this country. The A&B Writers' Guides list needs a book on *HOW TO WRITE NON-FICTION BOOKS*. This is it.

I estimate that the book will be 40-45,000 words long and have five or six line illustrations (supplied); it will be carefully 'tailored' to fit A&B's preferred 144 book-page format.

I expect to be able to deliver the completed book within about four months from signing the Agreement.

I am particularly well-qualified to write this book. I have written more than twenty adult non-fiction books and nine for children. My adult books range from traffic engineering to management techniques and . . . how to write; for children, from dinosaurs and superstitions to computers and social studies. A list of my books is attached.

....

Gordon Wells
[Date, etc.]

Fig 3.1 An example of a proposal (without the accompanying synopsis, – for this book

be used for the back-cover blurb – to persuade potential readers to buy the book. Put all you've got into it. It's really important.

Figure 3.1 reproduces (a slightly edited version of) the actual proposal that I submitted for this book.

A check list for the sales package

When you have completed your sales package – proposal plus synopsis – check it out against this list:

1 Have you come up with a short, catchy, descriptive title?
2 Have you clearly identified the target reader?
3 Have you explained why the reader will want to read your book?
4 Have you described the book (in both proposal and synopsis) in the best possible terms? Have you presented a good product image?
5 Have you explained – convincingly – why you are ideally qualified to write the book?
6 Does the synopsis make clear the content of each chapter and of the book as a whole?
7 Does the synopsis contain sufficient subject matter for a book (minimum say 30,000 words) – but not too much? (You're proposing a book, not a trilogy.)
8 Have you covered the whole of the subject, or should you consider reducing your intended scope to match the achievable coverage?
9 If the book subject is associated with an examination syllabus or the like, are you sure, and have you clearly stated, that the book will meet all its requirements?
10 Have you listed the competitive books and explained how and why yours will be better – or at least a valuable alternative?

Next, what to do with your honed and polished sales package.

4

SELLING THE IDEA

The sales package complete, we now have our 'something concrete' to sell. (And again, remember: a non-fiction book should preferably be 'sold' before it is written.) We have identified the overall market for the book. The market for the sales package is different; it can only be sold to one publisher. But which one?

Not all publishers will be interested in the type of book you propose. Your first task is to list all those who might be interested; then from that list, persuade one to publish it. A good place to start reviewing potential publishers is to see who has published other books on the same general subject. If your book is not in direct competition with one of their existing books they may be interested. (Sometimes, if your book is really different – or controversial – even if it does compete with an existing title, a publisher may still be interested.)

Researching publishers

List the publishers of the books (on the same or similar subjects) on your own shelves. Extend this list by looking in bookshops and libraries. With the more 'technical' book subjects the resultant list will seldom be long. With 'storyline' type books you will probably need to look more carefully: many publishers publish biographies and so-called 'general non-fiction' – you will need to investigate the areas and 'weight' of such books. (There is a major difference between the biography of pop-star Hubert Pumpernickel and that of the great King Cedric of Ruritania; the publisher of one will often not touch the other.)

Pay particular attention to the smaller, sometimes specialist publishers; not every good book is published by the giants. Conversely, don't shy completely away from the major publishing houses; they are just as keen to publish good new non-fiction books as are the smaller publishers. (Unfortunately though, bigger publishers are increasingly unwilling to consider proposals other than through literary agents. For more about agents, *see* Chapter 10.)

The two annual reference books, *The Writers' & Artists' Yearbook* (A. & C. Black) and *The Writer's Handbook* (Macmillan) are also useful for researching possible publishers. Both books list virtually every book publisher in the United Kingdom (and many overseas publishers too), giving addresses, names of directors, and the broad areas in which they specialise.

The very comprehensiveness of the two annuals means that details are restricted to just a few lines per publisher. A typical 'catch-all' entry might specify a publisher's areas of interest as:

Fiction, biography, illustrated, reference, travel.

Or, slightly more helpful, for non-fiction only:

History, natural history, health, biography, food and drink, crafts, gardening, poetry.

These are both actual entries. Clearly, they cover a multitude . . . Which, of course, is the intention: a good publisher will always expand his interests to accommodate an attractive-looking proposal.

More useful is my own *biennial* listing of publishers – *The Book Writer's Handbook* – in this, the Allison & Busby Writers' Guides series. Covering many fewer – but only 'relevant' – publishers, in much more detail, the *Handbook* outlines each publisher's areas of interest by listing many typical titles. It also indicates how each publisher prefers to be approached with new ideas – both fiction and non-fiction.

Of particular value too are each year's two special issues of *The Bookseller* magazine: the Spring and Autumn Books issues. Your local librarian probably gets copies – they may be in the library's reference section. Most booksellers too get copies – but may be less willing to let you browse for any length of time. These two bumper (500+ pages) volumes list (and sometimes describe) virtually every new book being published in the United Kingdom in the following six months, classified by subject areas. There are also advertisements of forthcoming books by most of the major publishers.

(You can, as I do, buy your own regular copies of the two bumper issues from the publishers, J. Whitaker & Sons Ltd, 12 Dyott Street, London WC1A 1DF – but the two-issue-only subscription costs over £30 a year.)

Once you have identified a number of potential publishers for your proposed book, it's worth studying the catalogues of your possible front-runners. Send a large (C4 sized, the envelope-equivalent of A4 paper) stamped addressed envelope – but it is difficult to know how much postage to affix. (The 100 gm rate is probably a good bet.) Or phone them – you might get the catalogue without sending the sae.

The catalogues will tell you much more about the publisher's books in the same general area as yours. You may be able to discern an underlying pattern in their books which might preclude or encourage yours. Look particularly for existing book series into which yours – perhaps amended – could fit. Fitting your book into an existing series will please the publisher – who will like the series to expand regularly – and be better for you, the author. Series of books tend to encourage serial sales.

From all your market research, sort your list into order. Approach, first, the publisher you think most likely to accept your book. (Or perhaps, start with the publisher by whom you would most like to be published – not necessarily the same one.)

Approaching publishers

You are now ready to write to your first-choice publisher. Yes, even if you live just around the corner from his office, write to him. You are trying to sell your idea for a book; books consist of written words. It's your written work the publisher needs to look at. Not you.

You may have the most sexy or manly (or both?) voice imaginable, but don't telephone about your book idea. Even if you are Miss World or Mr Universe, don't call in person asking to speak to the publisher.

Post your submission – sales package plus covering letter – or, if you must, just hand it to the receptionist ... and walk away.

Your letter, and the complete sales package as described in the previous chapter, will of course be typed. (More on presentation in Chapter 8.) Anything handwritten will barely get a cursory glance before certain rejection. Life is too short for publishers to waste time deciphering even the most legible of handwriting. If that means they accidentally miss out on your best-seller, there'll probably be something just as good – and typewritten – arriving tomorrow.

Nowadays, when most aspiring non-fiction authors use a word processor, it's easy. Print out a fresh copy for submission to each new publisher and a draft quality copy for your own records. If you're still working with a typewriter, type the sales package out – immaculately – and make several photocopies for submission. Type a fresh covering letter for each submission.

The covering letter accompanying the sales package can be brief; everything important is in the sales package. When approaching a new-to-me publisher with a book idea, I say something like:

Dear Mr Bloggs *

I am writing to enquire whether you might be interested in a new book about widget collecting. My working title is WIDGETS OF THE WESTERN WORLD. I believe it will fit snugly into your 'Collecting ...' series.

I enclose a brief note about the book, including an assessment of the possible market for it, the competing books, and my own 'credentials' for writing it, together with a detailed synopsis.

Needless to say, I would be willing to consider varying the synopsis should you feel this to be necessary.

If the idea interests you, you will no doubt wish to see sample chapters. Chapters 2 and 3 are virtually complete **; I could let you have copies of these within days of an expression of interest.

I enclose a stamped addressed envelope for your reply.

Yours sincerely

Gordon Wells

* Address someone at the publisher's office by name. Unless you already have the name of a contact person, telephone the firm and ask the operator for the name of the editorial director.

** It's better that *you* specify the chapters you have ready (even if they aren't quite) – that way you can choose those aspects on which you are most *up to speed*. If not, the publisher may ask to see specific chapters which, this early on, you are less ready to write.

Notice the final paragraph in the covering letter – about the stamped addressed envelope. Publishers receive large numbers of unsolicited submissions each week; the return postage bill – for wholly non-profit-making rejections of unwanted and largely unsuitable material – can be huge. The stamped addressed envelope makes it more likely that you will get a reply; most – but sadly not all, these days – publishers are polite enough to do that. No sae makes a reply much less likely.

Multiple submissions

It is appropriate to mention the growing practice of multiple submissions: submitting your book idea to several publishers at the same time. Some years ago, such a practice, once discovered, would be the kiss of death for an author. Publishers liked (like) to take their time when considering an idea. They dislike the pressure of competing against a deadline for a decision.

Today, the practice of multiple submissions is widely adopted and, grudgingly, accepted. The multiple submission approach means that the author doesn't have to wait two or three months again and again as one publisher after the other rejects a marginal idea. (Really rotten ideas usually get a quicker brush-off.)

If you believe that there are a lot of suitable publishers who might be interested in your book-idea, then multiple submission may be the right approach. But – it is essential that each of the publishers to whom you simultaneously submit your sales package is aware that others are also considering it. It's worth repeating that, for emphasis:

IF MAKING MULTIPLE SUBMISSIONS – LET THE PUBLISHERS KNOW

It is debatable whether or not you should/need divulge the names of the several considering publishers – certainly it would be polite; it is also a matter for consideration whether or not you should specify a deadline for decisions before you offer the idea to another batch of possible publishers.

As soon as one of the several publishers makes an offer to publish your book, you should notify the other publishing houses and withdraw it from offer. (Unless everyone knows it's an auction – but that's an unexplored world for most non-fiction authors.)

Personally, I have not yet found it necessary or desirable to make multiple submission offers to publishers; most of my books are of relatively narrow interest. Follow my lead if you wish – but be aware of the possibility of multiple submissions.

Multiple or single submission though, once the letter(s) and sales package are despatched, forget them as best you can. You've got lots more research to do – and all those household chores you've been putting off while you worked on the synopsis. Don't expect a speedy reply; after a month, you could try a delicate reminder, 'enquiring whether there is any news'. You might follow this up with a courteous telephone enquiry.

If you haven't heard within two months you have to decide whether to send a further, perhaps slightly more forceful, reminder – or withdraw the idea from offer to that publisher. A long delay might mean that several people are reading and seriously considering your idea; it could equally easily mean that there is a large backlog of unsolicited material and a 'snowed-under' reader.

It's often best just to sit it out – with frequent reminders.

Rejection

Prepare yourself. Your sales package may be rejected. Don't be too upset by this. I doubt whether there is a non-fiction author around who hasn't had book-ideas rejected . . . by the first publisher.

Rejections come in various forms: there is the cold and impersonal 'Not for us, thanks' form; and then there's the 'What a good idea but I'm afraid our list is full for the next couple of years' type. You might get back a letter saying something like 'I wish we could take it but we're full up; try Blanks, they're just starting a new series that this looks ideal for'. I had a 'try Blanks' rejection once. I tried Blanks ... and quickly got a contract for the book. On the whole, most people in the publishing world are kind and helpful – but frantically busy. If they take the trouble to offer advice, it's usually worth following up. But even then, don't hold your breath.

Blunt or encouraging though, a rejection is a rejection is a rejection. It is never what you want. But you should never be too disheartened by rejection. You've got to ride it out.

(My idea for what was to become *How to Communicate* – and now, as a revised third edition for my Singapore publisher, *Effective Communication* – was rejected by a dozen publishers before McGraw-Hill asked me to widen the scope I had planned on. Then they accepted it. They kept it going through two revised editions before letting it go and allowing the rights to revert to me. For more on Agreements, rights, etc. *see* Chapter 10.)

When you get a rejection letter, curse, take a deep breath and resubmit the sales package to the second of your preferred publishers. And if he rejects it, resubmit to number three, and so on. Apart from helping you to survive the rejection pains, resubmission keeps the idea out 'on offer'.

If you get several rapid rejections, stop and think. Did any publishers explain their reasons – if so, is there a common theme? Think about it. Otherwise, possible reasons for rejection include:

- the idea is lousy – is it?
- the package does not present the idea well – doesn't it?
- all the publishers are over-stocked for their future programmes – unlikely, except in a recession.
- all the publishers are stupid or blind – that is, everyone is 'out of step' except you. No. Most publishers are astute business people or they'd soon go out of business. But they CAN make mistakes.
- there are already enough books on the market on the subject – did you fall down in your market research?

● there is no market for the idea – is it too esoteric?
● you are trying the wrong publishers – faulty market research again?

Assuming that after your rethink you remain convinced that the idea is worth proceeding with, that there is a market for it, and that the sales package presents the idea as well as possible, off you go again. (Don't be put off if you hear that another book on the same subject is being prepared by another author. It is unlikely that both will cover exactly the same ground.) Submit the sales package to the next publisher in the list.

If I were convinced that my idea was good I would not give up until I'd been rejected perhaps twenty times. (And possibly not even then, if I could still see some more likely publishers.)

But let's be more optimistic. Fairly soon, one of your preferred publishers shows interest. You might get a phone call asking you to come and discuss the project; more likely, you will receive a letter asking to see a couple of sample chapters – ideally, agreeing to look at the ones you've mentioned. The publisher needs the sample chapters to assure himself that you know how to write: you may have put together an excellent synopsis and proposal but turn out not to be much good at explaining, teaching or 'storytelling'.

Sample chapters

The sample chapters that you now have to complete must be the very best you are capable of. They are your . . . samples. A lot will hang on how they impress the publisher: for their clarity, their 'easy readability', their coverage.

They must be complete in every respect: if the finished book is to have illustrations, worked examples, exercises – so must the samples. And don't keep the publisher waiting too long for them. You want to get back to him while he's still interested and enthusiastic. Don't give him time to forget you and your interesting idea; there's always another interesting-looking book-idea about to land on his desk.

There will be detailed advice on the organisation, mechanics and process of writing and presenting non-fiction in the next few chapters. You need to take all of this advice on board when preparing your samples. Read the whole of this book before you charge off into the publishing jungle.

If you are using a typewriter, I would recommend – for the sample chapters only – submitting photocopies of the finished typescript; add a brief note in the covering letter to the effect that you are preserving the 'top typescript copy' for final and complete delivery. If using a word processor there is no problem – submit a top copy and be prepared to print it out again later.

As with the sales package, post the sample chapters – addressed by name to the person you are now dealing with. Enclose a stamped addressed envelope (but now, this'll probably be returned unused). Enclose a further, small, stamped self-addressed envelope and ask for an acknowledgement of receipt.

You should get an acknowledgement fairly quickly – within a week or so. Don't expect a final decision on the sample chapters that quickly though. The editor will be dealing with a number of book projects, all at different stages, all at the same time. She will read the samples as soon as she can. (Note that henceforth, for convenience, I call editors 'she' – which term includes male editors too.) But she will not be the only person to read them. It's most likely that the samples, together with your initial sales package, will also be sent to one or more readers – one, possibly an expert on the subject of your book – for comments. The readers' comments are not the sole decisive factor in whether or not your book goes ahead; but they are undoubtedly important.

Let's assume that the comments are favourable. The editor will now probably decide that she would like to meet you, for a general and wide-ranging discussion of your book idea. You're close to a firm acceptance now.

Figure 4.1 shows, in flow chart format, the overall process from sales package submission to publication date.

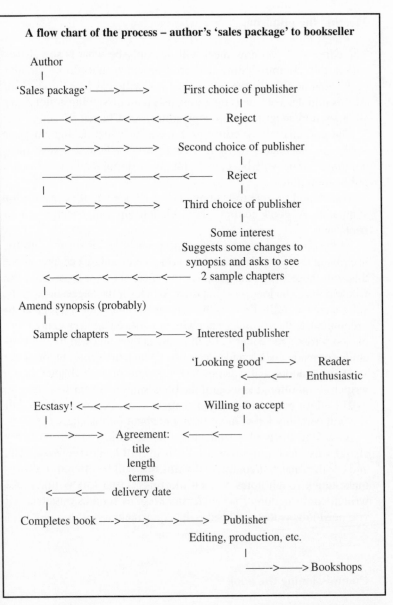

Figure 4.1 A flow-chart showing the process from author's preparation of the 'sales package' to the delivery of the finished typescript to the publisher.

Meeting the publisher

The editor that you now meet will probably be what is sometimes called the commissioning editor. She may indeed, in smaller publishing houses, be the *only* editor you will deal with throughout. At this initial stage, she is operating as a commissioning editor; later she may transmogrify into a copy editor (*see* Chapter 9).

The commissioning editor will have to justify taking on your book; she may have to fight its case at an editorial board; once committed, she will be closely involved throughout your book's publication process.

You should be able to lean on her for advice and if necessary for sympathy. A good editor/author relationship can become a real friendship.

At this first meeting, the editor will probably offer suggestions for improving the synopsis: extend the scope here, add in a chapter about this, run those two 'thin' chapters together. She may even want the whole book to be longer – or shorter. Whatever the suggestions, consider them carefully. Discuss the reasons for them and be prepared to accommodate them – or explain why not. The editor sees many more books, across a far wider field, than any author, and will have a better idea of market needs and saleability. (With a first-time author, some – a few – editors will welcome/ask for sight of each chapter as it's written – and offer guidance on the book's development.)

The editor may not know much about your specialist subject, but she will certainly know more than you about publishing.

As well as the book's content and framework, you will probably also discuss such important details as overall length, delivery date, and . . . the financial/contractual terms that will be offered. I always make quick rough notes at such meetings – and follow up with a written confirmation *of my understanding*, as soon as possible. All you need now is the go-ahead – the Agreement.

Commissioning the book

Unless the commissioning editor has been able to give you the go-ahead at your meeting – at a small publishing house, likely; at a larger one, unlikely – you must now wait a little longer. An added advantage of your writing to confirm what was agreed at your meeting is that you may thereby provoke a letter advising you that 'an Agreement is being prepared'. Given such a letter, I would start work without waiting for the Agreement.

The Agreement, and associated matters – advances, royalties, etc. – are examined in some detail in Chapter 10. For now, it is sufficient that the publisher agrees to publish your book providing that you deliver it to him by an agreed date. The publisher contracts to pay you a royalty – a percentage of the book's sale price – for each copy sold. And the publisher should pay you a partial advance against those future royalties as soon as you sign the Agreement. That is, you should get some money 'up front'.

Once the Agreement is signed by both you and the publisher, you must get down to work in earnest on your book. You are (both) committed. You are committed to a delivery date that you will have discussed and agreed with the editor. Perhaps more important, you are committed to a finished length – also pre-agreed.

The publisher prepares his publishing programme many months in advance; he will arrange production schedules – copy editing, typesetting, printing and binding . . . and publicity – all along the line. If the author delivers late the production schedule is upset; the publisher incurs extra costs and publication is delayed. If the author delivers a short or over-long book, this too can upset the whole costing basis on which the book was accepted.

You MUST work to time and to length. Advice on this is included in the next chapter.

What if the book is 'sold' to you?

So far in this book we have been considering the author with a book-idea who seeks to persuade someone to accept and publish it. There is another scenario. Sometimes – particularly for 'technical' books – the need for a book is perceived by the publisher. The publisher seeks out a suitable person to write the book for him. If you are a recognised expert in some field, the 'suitable person' sought out by the publisher could be you. What do you do?

A similar situation can arise in the field of children's non-fiction; some publishers have lists of experienced children's authors. The editorial staff come up with a book idea . . . and ask one of their favoured writers to work on it for them. Again, what's to do?

The commissioned author is in much the same position as the author with an idea to sell – but with much of the uncertainty removed. The publisher wants a book on the subject and wants you to write it. All you have to do is justify the publisher's need and faith.

You still need to do much of what has already been described. Specifically you should:

- investigate competing texts – to see how they handle the subject
- motivate yourself to write the book – think it through
- assure yourself – and the commissioning editor – that you can cover the whole subject (or, perhaps that you can persuade a colleague to help fill in the gaps in your knowledge)
- together with the commissioning editor, define the target reader.
- prepare the synopsis and obtain editorial agreement
- think about – and check/discuss with the commissioning editor – a suitable title
- write sample chapters. If you have not previously worked for the publisher before, he will need assurance of your writing skills

From here on, everything in this book applies equally to the author who seeks out the publisher and to the author approached by the publisher. No matter from which side you approach the writing grindstone, your nose will be in the same extended contact with it.

Finally, in respect of commissioned books, there is the specialist task of compiling and editing multi-contribution books – usually very technical or academic books. A specialist might approach an academic/specialist publisher with an idea for a coherent compilation of specialist contributions; more likely, a publisher will ask a well-known expert to compile such a book. We look (a little) further at such an editorial role in Chapter 6.

5

ORGANISING THE WRITING

The book idea is sold; now you have to produce it. Before offering some advice on the actual writing of non-fiction books, let's consider the organisation – the mechanics of it all.

We have already produced the synopsis for the book. But this is never final, nor has it always been considered in sufficient detail at the 'within-chapter' level. Now is the time to do that: to arrange the chapter contents into their 'best', most logical sequence. It is the logical structure of book and chapter that carries the reader along, understanding and enjoying.

Organisation – in all its manifestations – is an essential part of the non-fiction author's job.

Organising the chapter content

By organising our book in more-or-less self-contained chapters we make the task of writing the book more manageable; we are bringing everything down to an understandable scale. We need only think about one chapter at a time – a mere four or five thousand words.

Let's make the task seem even simpler. We do this by looking in more detail at each chapter's proposed content. For the chapter you are now reading, my original (overall) synopsis was:

The mechanics of writing: Expanding the synopsis into chapter skeletons. Developing within-chapter logic. Counting words ('Writer is someone who counts words.' Braine). Working to a word budget – leading to agreed book-length. Importance of a hierarchy of headings. How many drafts? Word processing. Regularity – writing routine. Linking text and illustrations. Other writing equipment.

It's all there, but it's useful to expand it somewhat before actually writing. And the organisation – the logical sequence – needs to be carefully reviewed.

Even though nowadays I do all my work on a word processor, I still find it easiest to do my book- and chapter-planning in 'longhand' (actually, more like 'scribbles') on paper. I take a sheet of A4 and write out the synopsis subjects in a list spread down the page, leaving plenty of space around them. Then, thinking hard, I expand on the headings, noting down the points I want to make. The points seldom come to me in order – there are always afterthoughts, and many changes of mind. (I must remember to mention writer's block – I've just read an interesting article about it.)

While thinking about the points to include, I also review the logic of their order. Should I start with the word budget or with the arrangement? Should I mention the need for regular writing before or after I suggest the equipment that might be needed? Does the point about thinking of illustrations belong in this chapter – or in the next? Arrows criss-cross the page; notes to myself abound. And maybe I come up with an idea for the opening paragraph – always important. That's scribbled down on the page too, so that I don't forget it.

There are computer programs that will help you organise the content of a book or chapter. If you are happy working that way, fine. You'll end up with much the same result as I get from my on-page 'doodles'. (I see little point in using special programs anyway: you can insert and/or move phrases around with any word processor program – which is all that's needed.)

Figure 5.1 reproduces the notes I made while planning this chapter. It also shows how my ideas about the order of the contents changed as I thought the sequence through.

Notice the target wordage for each section within the chapter. Not only does this afford a check on the overall chapter length but also on the balance of words per section.

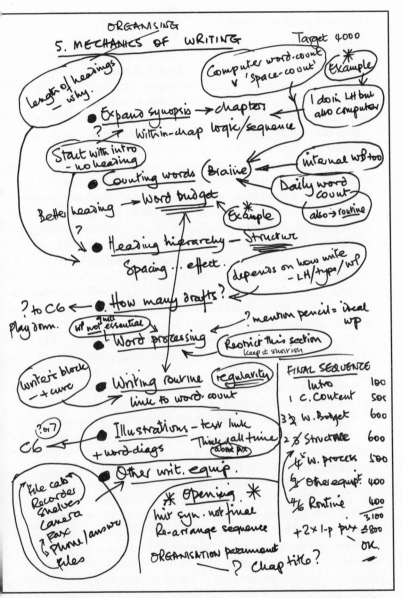

Figure 5.1 A reproduction of the scribbled notes from which I worked while writing this chapter

Organising the structure

In the 'technical' type of non-fiction book, it helps if the organisation of the (book and) chapter structure is clear to the reader. Section headings are like signposts; they help the reader find the way around. They help the reader to relocate a section of particular interest; they warn of what's ahead. And, just as road signs are standardised, so too should the headings follow a recognisable hierarchical convention.

Nothing is more amateurish, and distracting to the reader, than inexplicable changes in the heading hierarchy. By that I mean when a chapter starts with simple, one-stage headings (lower-case characters say, aligned to the left margin) and then, after a page or two, descends to a second stage (centred capitals, say) – and then continues using the second-stage headings throughout the rest of the chapter.

The reader is left wondering whether the later headings are subsidiary to the early first-stage ones or not. (Usually, the first two or three second-level headings are correctly second-level; then the author forgets the original hierarchy, and the rest of the headings should have been first-level ones.)

These nonsenses seldom get past a competent copy-editor – but you occasionally find them in academic papers . . . and often in typescripts.

Inconsistency in maintaining a hierarchy of headings only demonstrates an author's inability to organise his/her thoughts and writing.

A non-fiction author should nearly always be able to manage (and this only in the more 'technical' of books) with chapter titles and two further levels of heading. (In most non-fiction books, a single level of within-chapter headings should suffice – as in this book.)

Headings – both chapter titles and within-chapter headings – should be kept fairly short – aim at no more than half-a-dozen words. The main chapter titles are often used as *running heads*: page headings. (The book title is usually on the left hand page, the chapter title on the right hand.) If chapter titles are too long, they will spread right across the page – or beyond – which doesn't look good. The shorter the within-chapter heading, the more blank space around it, the more it stands out on the page. It's a more useful signpost.

The more within-chapter headings you use, the more the book-pages are split up, the easier to read and more understandable the book appears. Use frequent headings in introductory, popular, 'How To' books; less frequently in heavier tomes. I usually aim to have at *least* one heading on each double-page spread of the finished book (ie. a maximum of about a thousand words apart); when writing for a younger readership I use headings as frequently as every 2-300 words.

And a personal note: a chapter should never start with a heading – it moves the text-proper too low down and it looks awkward. I recommend at least one or two introductory paragraphs before a first heading.

Organising the output – the word budget

Of equal importance to the organisation and sub-division of each chapter's content is the length of each section and chapter. You are committed to a book of an agreed length. And the length, as far as the author is concerned, is measured in words.

As the novelist John Braine says in his book *Writing a Novel*, 'a writer is a person who counts words'. Unless you count your words, you don't know how your output compares with the total requirement. (Word counting can help generate an improvement in writing style too – *see* Chapter 6.)

When preparing the synopsis, we thought in terms of about ten chapters of about 4,000 words each. When doing the more detailed within-chapter planning, we mentioned the need for the topics to be treated in a balanced way – it's no good enthusiastically writing 3000 words about one of half-a-dozen or more topics and then trying to deal with the other five in the remaining 1000 or so words. The detailed planning may lead us to vary the standard chapter length – but within the overall book total. For these and other reasons (including your writing routine), the non-fiction author should count words.

One way – I think the best – of keeping a check on the overall book length while maintaining the between- and within-chapter balance is to establish a word budget. Figure 5.2 shows the word budget to which I worked in writing this book – and how I lived up to it.

HOW TO WRITE NON-FICTION BOOKS   Progress/word budget

| First draft | | | | | | | Second draft | | |
Chap	Target	Run Tot	Actual	Run Tot	EndP	EndDate	RevWds	EndP	RevTot
NTRO	3000	3000	3220	3220	10	050195	3150	10	3150
01	2000	5000	2120	5340	16	060195	2070	16	5220
02	4000	9000	4660	10000	30	140195	4330	29	9550
03	4000	13000	5270	15270	45	180195	5120	44/5	14670
04	4000	17000	4300	19570	58/9	200195	4110	57/8	18780
05	4000	21000	3280	22850	68/71	230195	3150	67/9	21930
06	4000	25000	4120	26970	83	250195	4100	81	26030
07	4000	29000	2670	29640	92	260195	2400	89/90	28430
08	4000	33000	4390	34030	104	300195	4300	102	32730
09	4000	37000	3230	37260	113/4	010295	3180	111/2	35910
10	5000	42000	5740	43000	131	050295	5590	129	41500
Apdx1	1000	43000	460	43460	133	060295	460	131	41960
Apdx2	1000	44000	730	44190	135	060295	720	133	42680
Apdx3	500	44500	260	44450	136	060295	260	134	42940
Indx									

Progress

Date	Chap	EndWds	DayWds	RunTot
040195	00	1100	1100	1100
050195	00	3040/	1940	3220
060195	01	2120/	2120	5340
090195	02	990	990	6330
110195	02	2260	1270	7600
120195	02	3960	1700	9300
140195	02	4660/	700	10000
150195	03	540	540	10540
160195	03	1400	860	11400
170195	03	2890	1490	12890
180195	03	5270/	2380	15270
190195				

Figure 5.2 The word budget for this book – showing how the actual wordage varied from the chapter targets, yet balanced out overall.

You know the total book length – from which you must not significantly vary; you know the chapter contents (and likely lengths – which you can vary); you know there are going to be extras – appendices, etc. Make a table showing each chapter, etc. and its planned length; ensure that this adds up to the agreed total length – or replan until it does. Refer back to Figure 5.1 also: the numbers against the sequence-list are a simplied within-chapter word budget.

Your word budget is not cast in stone though. It is only a target. Some chapters will inevitably run out over-length – and others short. As long as the running total is about right, small variations are unimportant. But if *all* the chapters are longer than planned you must do some serious thinking. Are you waffling? Can you trim back at the second or third draft stage? An over-long (or over-short) book can negate all the financial calculations the publisher made in determining the viability of the book. If you can see no way out of this difficulty . . . contact your editor and discuss it as soon as possible.

It is also useful to count words to check your overall progress. Am I writing sufficient words per day to meet the delivery deadline? Checking on daily output also becomes a minor spur to achievement: can I produce more words today than I did yesterday? Other times I tell myself that I cannot stop . . . until I have met my daily target.

How do you count the words – surely not one by one? I believe that a beginner is well advised to do just that – on occasions I still do that myself – for it gives a better *feel* for the way one is writing. (Friends tell me that I am near-paranoid about word-counting though, so maybe that's a mite over-fussy.) If drafting in longhand, or direct on a typewriter though, I would determine the average words per page or line and calculate daily output from that. If working with a word processor, the word-count can usually be determined automatically.

(My own word processor program, Quill, from Psion's PC-4 suite, is the only one I know which gives a permanently-on-screen, running word-count. Each time I press the space-bar after a word or just one character, the word-count at the bottom of the screen goes up by one.)

When it comes to the overall book length, though, the word count that the publisher wants is one based on space occupied rather than a computer figure. To derive the word-count wanted by the publisher, count the words on a full page of your own typescript – standard number of lines per page, and no headings or other space-extravagances – and multiply by the number of pages. In other words the space-count takes the blank spaces – at chapter start and finish, etc. – into account.

Organising yourself – a writing routine

As already hinted at above, you should be regular in your writing habits. Anyone who writes only when the muse moves him/her is an amateur; the professional writes steadily and regularly, on 'good' and 'bad' days alike. Regularity tends to make the words flow a little easier; it keeps the *writing muscle* exercised and fit.

Some authors decide that they will write for so many hours a day; others set themselves a target number of words. I belong to the latter school.

When I was a wage-slave, commuting daily to London, I aimed at writing 400 words every day (on weekdays, in the evening for an hour after dinner) plus an extra thousand over the weekend: nearly a chapter a week. Now that I write full-time, I set myself a readily achievable target of 800 words per day, minimum, on a book project – plus all my regular and irregular articles, etc. And of course, these target output figures exclude the time needed for planning, research, redrafting, and all the business matters associated with authorship. Given the facts at my fingertips, I can now do the first draft of an adult non-fiction book in about two months.

I keep a record of my daily output on the same computer file or sheet of paper as my word budget. The lower part of Figure 5.2 shows part of the progress record for this book.

A non-fiction author working to the system I advocate in this book – detailed book and chapter synopses and regular writing – should never suffer from *writer's block*. (*Writer's block* is when the words just won't come. I believe it is more of a novelist's complaint – and then mostly for those writing 'literary' fiction, without the

– and then mostly for those writing 'literary' fiction, without the preliminary synopsis used by many *genre* writers.)

If you have inertia trouble getting started each day, some hints:

● Start with an easy chapter – or part of the chapter. With a detailed synopsis you don't need to write in sequence. (It's often sensible to write the important introductory chapter *last*, when you know exactly what to . . . introduce.)

● When you stop writing each day, leave a note for yourself of what is to come next – the next few words or the next subject. Stop in mid-sentence. Next day, re-read the previous two or three paragraphs and then, with the note, you'll be away.

● If you're really stuck, read what one of the competitive books had to say on your next subject. You can do better than that!

While actually writing, don't worry overmuch if a sentence won't come right. Write it as best you can – and come back to it. It's more important to keep the flow of words and ideas moving than to perfect one sentence. More about polishing in the next chapter.

Processing the words

The actual writing – putting the words together in the best sequence – is the subject of the next chapter. It follows naturally from a working routine, though, to consider the equipment that a non-fiction author needs. This raises the question of a word processor.

If you are serious about writing your non-fiction book, you will probably – and wisely – have learnt much of your trade already, by writing feature articles. You may have earned enough to finance the purchase of a word processor. A word processor is not an essential piece of equipment for a non-fiction author . . . but life is immeasurably easier with one.

If you've got a typewriter and can't afford a word processor – don't worry. The only essential is that your work is in typescript.

Very briefly, a word processor is a program which enables a computer to . . . process words. (You'll need a printer too.)

Using a computer plus word processor program – usually referred to collectively as a word processor – you type (using a near-conventional keyboard) and your words appear on a television-like screen before you. Every now and then – and certainly before you stop work for any reason – you can *save* your work: much like making a tape-recording except that the recording medium is a disk.

Once your work is saved, the computer can be switched off. Some time later, the machine is switched on again, the saved work can be *loaded* back into the computer, and your words will reappear on the screen. If you wish, you can erase a character, a word, a sentence – or more – on the screen and substitute your new preference. If you want to rearrange the sequence of sentences or paragraphs, this too is easy.

Once you've 'got it right' you re-*save* it, then press a few keys and the printer prints it out on paper for you. You'll look at this *hard copy* (to differentiate from the electronic or 'soft' copy on the disk) and find still more changes that need making. No problem, *reload* the work from the disk, correct it on the screen, *resave* it . . . and print out a fresh copy. You can even have the computer check your text for spelling errors – syntax too in some programs.

Writing on a word processor is easier than on a typewriter – quicker too; you don't need to worry about typing errors, they are so easily corrected. But there is a 'down' side to word processing: it encourages 'verbal diarrhoea' – excess waffling. But once aware of the possibility of over-writing, you can guard against it.

Don't be scared of word processors; they're easy to use. You can learn the basics in an hour or so. It's only computer buffs and salesmen who make them sound complicated. And once you're working with one, you'll never go back. But an author needs more than just a word processor.

Other equipment

Either a typewriter or a word processor is an absolute essential for any author. If for no other reason, because it costs too much to hire a typist. But, as stressed at the start of this chapter, the non-fiction author must be organised. For that, other items of equipment will help – some more than others. There are essentials, and there are things that one would like to have but can manage without.

Let's review necessities and niceties:

- Files – a necessity. You will need to file your research material (*see* Chapter 2), your correspondence (which grows inexorably), and all the drafts of the book in hand – and those to follow. I recommend lever-arch files for research and correspondence and card files (buy in bulk) for book manuscripts. You'll also need a filing punch and a small stapler.
- Bookshelves – a virtual necessity. A non-fiction author collects facts – in books and the aforementioned files. You can't stack them on the floor for ever . . . the stacks fall over. I recommend the adjustable shelves that fit on multi-position metal wall-supports.
- Filing cabinet – at first a nicety, soon a necessity. Initially, store files in the bookshelves.
- Camera – almost, if not quite, a necessity. Even if you're not a skilled photographer – and it's not difficult these days – a camera is an ideal way of recording scenes, etc. It is also useful for copying reference book pages etc. when there's no photocopier handy.
- Cassette recorder – unless you are doing a lot of interviewing when it's a necessity, this is a nicety.
- Telephone – a virtual necessity these days. And an answer-phone comes close to essential too.
- Fax machine – a high-priority nicety. (I went for a long while thinking I didn't really need one; now I know I did.)
- Letter scales – a nicety. But mine has saved me many walks to the local post office to weigh a parcel of typescript. (This would be an ideal thing to put on your Christmas present list.)

6

THE WRITING ITSELF

I notice that you use plain, simple language, short words and brief sentences. That is the way to write English. It is the modern way and the best way. Stick to it.

Mark Twain

This book is not written for the literary genius; he/she needs no help from me – nor would I aspire to offer it. It is written for the ordinary person, capable of writing, but perhaps not quite as fluently as they might wish. The sort of person who would appreciate a few helpful guidelines.

The first piece of advice about writing style is . . . don't worry. The non-fiction author – particularly of 'technical' type books – doesn't have to write great literature; the purpose of the non-fiction author is to write so that the reader can understand. Indeed, the less a personal writing style is apparent, the better the writing. The most effective non-fiction authors are those who are, to all intents and purposes, *transparent*: their writing style does not noticeably come between them and their readers.

It is easy to advise aspiring authors that the way to write well is to practise. That is, of course, correct – but it doesn't help much. Writing style can also be improved by exposure to good writing. That too is good advice – but what is good writing? Most reading – both non-fiction and fiction – is helpful to an aspiring author. But the author of 'technical' type non-fiction books should be wary of some of the colourful descriptive passages appropriate in some fiction. Colourful description is often useful in the 'storyline' type of non-fiction; it is seldom appropriate in 'technical' non-fiction –

floweriness can get in the way of communication. Effective, 'readable' non-fiction writing – both for 'technical' and for 'storyline' type books – is not easy. You have to work hard at making it a welcoming and easy read. Sheridan got it right when he said, 'You write with ease, to show your breeding, but easy writing's curst hard reading'.

Stylistic guidelines

While writing style must always be a matter of personal choice, there are a few guidelines – not 'rules', merely guidance – that will help. Break them intentionally, if you will – but never by accident. In summary, the basic writing guidelines for non-fiction authors are:

● always think of and write for the target reader
● make sure your writing is always accurate
● keep your writing brief – as tight and concise as possible
● ensure that your writing is clear and simple – easy to understand

Think of the last three of those guidelines as the ABC of writing: your writing should always be A-accurate, B-brief and C-clear.

The most important thing for the non-fiction author to remember is to aim, always and specifically, at the target reader. Your purpose is to communicate with the reader; if the reader doesn't understand your explanations or gets bored by your descriptions, you're wasting your time – and theirs.

You must NEVER appear to be writing down to the reader. Nothing will do more to dissuade the uncommitted from buying or reading your book than an author's patronising attitude. You must write what the reader wants to read, not what you want to write. Think of your target reader – whether child or adult – as of equal intelligence to yourself; they are merely less aware than you of the particular subject. (You might use simpler words and more explanation when writing for children – but I prefer simple words anyway and the amount of explanation needed depends solely on where the reader is starting from.)

Remind yourself how little if anything you know about sheep farming or deep-sea diving or . . . If you were reading a book about those subjects you yourself would want the explanation to start from basics. Humility is an essential characteristic of a non-fiction author.

Accuracy

The reason for accuracy is obvious – but merits restating. A book is 'an authority'. For years, readers will refer to your book, treating its contents as fact – unless a statement therein is clearly differentiated as opinion. One silly little mistake can damn an otherwise authoritative volume. The research processes outlined in Chapter 2 should guard against such inaccuracy but you must always check . . . and check again.

The need for accuracy does not stop with the facts though. It is also important that what you have written is what you mean; it is all too easy to change the whole meaning of a sentence with a late-inserted clause. Are you absolutely certain of the meaning of that slightly unusual, nice-sounding word you've used? (Check the meaning in the dictionary and then – probably – replace it with a more readily understandable word. Your target reader won't always have a dictionary handy and words of uncertain meaning disturb the reading flow. But this is more to do with Clarity, see below.)

Check your spelling too. (Don't rely entirely on the spell-checker built into your word processor – that's the way Americanisms unintentionally slip in.) Time and again I find that my certainty about how to spell a supposedly well-known word is unfounded: I've only just realised that *desparate* – which I thought looked right – should be spelt *desperate*. A writer's dictionary should be well-thumbed (and up-to-date, but that's a different matter).

Brevity

Brevity is not really the right word for this particular advice on writing style – but it fits the ABC structure. A better word would be *concise* – in other words, without unnecessary words.

While overall shortness is a decided virtue in, for example, management writing, there is room to expand when writing a non-fiction book. But this does not mean that there is room for waffle or padding. Non-fiction writing has to be taut – free from superfluous words – yet expansive where detail is necessary. All of us can improve our writing by the judicious trimming of the odd word – or more.

But of equal or greater effect on writing style, the recommendation of Brevity is also applicable to words, sentences and paragraphs:

- Always use a short word in preference to a long word – even if this means that you need two or three short words to replace a single longer one. Short words are easier to understand than longer ones. Use words with which most people are familar. If you cannot avoid using a long/difficult word, ensure that the meaning is made clear – either by explanation or by its context.
- Keep sentences short – restricted to a single statement. Aim at an average sentence length of about 15 words – and a maximum length of 25 words. (For counting purposes, though, treat properly used semi-colons and colons as full stops.) But – most important – vary your sentence lengths; don't make them all about the average length. Remember: to maintain the 15-word average, a 25-word sentence has to be balanced with a 5-word one.

  I would not criticise long sentences merely because they are long; long sentences can be perfectly sensible and clear. But to write a good, long sentence entails care and skill; it's easier to write a good, readily understandable short sentence. And short sentences are easier to punctuate: commas and full-stops will usually suffice. The link between simplicity and clarity is further emphasised in the next section – on Clarity.
- Paragraphs should, when writing for book, rather than periodical, publication, be restricted to an average length of about 80 words and a maximum of perhaps 150. (In case you're checking, my own style, nurtured in the article-writing 'business', tends to end up rather shorter.)

There are two reasons for these length-limits: first, no paragraph should deal with more than a single thought – often propounded in the first sentence and elaborated on in subsequent sentences – which leads to short paragraphs; secondly, long paragraphs actually look as though they are going to be difficult to understand – even if they're not. Short paragraphs make readers feel better.

As with sentences, avoid a string of average-length paragraphs; vary the paragraph lengths for a good-looking page. An occasional short, 'tabloidy' paragraph enlivens the reader.

As you write, think about the lengths of your sentences and paragraphs. Do your paragraphs – in typescript – look long? There is nothing to stop you from sub-dividing a long-looking paragraph into two or more shorter ones – I've done it several times in this chapter already. (The 'rule' about 'one para, one thought' does not preclude such splitting, resulting in 'two paras, one thought'. What should be avoided is 'one para, two thoughts'.) When shortening paragraphs, though, remember the need for the end result to flow, rather than seem disjointed – *see* below, under Clarity.

Most of us, when we're not thinking about it, allow our sentences to ramble on. So think.

Watch out particularly for the word 'and' in mid-sentence; this can often, with considerable improvement in readability, be replaced by a full stop. Think too before you insert that qualifying clause in mid-sentence. Might it not be better as a separate sentence, immediately after its 'parent'?

Think too about the effect of a string of short or long sentences. Several short sentences in sequence will create a feeling of urgency and jumpiness (ideal in a thriller, less so in a non-fiction book); too many long sentences one after the other can generate a soporific effect – hence 'a boring book'.

It will be clear that the advice in this section adds weight to that in the previous chapter about counting words. Unless you count the words you write – and sentence by sentence, paragraph by paragraph, not just overall – it is easy to become long-winded without realising it. A long-winded writer is a less-than-effective writer. Counting words improves your style.

Clarity

The non-fiction author's purpose is to communicate, to convey information to the reader. Think always of your target reader; your message must be clear and unconfusing. It is only the inadequate, incompetent, or pompous writer who feels a need to wrap up his or her thoughts in deliberately confusing gobbledegook. Never seek to impress the reader with the extent of your knowledge or ability – nor to show how profound your thinking, or how literary your writing is.

The best way of writing clearly is to write simply. Think of English as one language – not as spoken English and written English – and *write like you talk.* (I acknowledge my debt to Robert Gunning's book *The Technique of Clear Writing*, for his less grammatical 'write like' rather than the correct, but less meaningful, 'write as'.)

As you write, think to yourself, 'Would I *say* it like that? Or would the listener's expression make it clear that I sounded pompous, wordy and/or unclear?'

A speaker has the advantage of instant visual feedback and can adjust the explanation level to make sure that the message is understood. The writer has no such feedback – further demonstrating the importance of having a clear concept of your target reader. A writer must write at just the right level for the reader to understand, but without 'talking down'. Strive for a smooth, non-flowery flow of words and thoughts. (I find it helpful to mutter my words to myself as I write them. And *see* below for the recommendation that, when checking and polishing, you should actually read your work out loud.)

But the advice to *write like you talk* needs to be taken with a pinch of salt. Many people speak English loosely, not finishing sentences and with many expressive pauses (while they think what to say next). Some people speak badly. What I am really advising is that you write *as you wish you spoke* – simply, confidently and expressively, using familiar words, but without excessive colloquialism.

If you *write like you talk* you will use mainly everyday words. Everyday words are short, simple and easy to understand – *see* Brevity.

Clarity is also enhanced by the use of simple punctuation – which goes hand-in-hand with the recommendation (under Brevity) to keep sentences short. The purpose of punctuation is to help make the writing clear. You should punctuate, therefore, only as much as is necessary to make the meaning clear. You will find that long sentences need a lot of punctuation; short sentences are already clear and are well served by commas and full stops alone. A comma indicates a pause, a full stop the end of a statement.

Colons and semi-colons are almost full stops; they are used to link two short, related – sometimes incomplete – statements. The colon is also the correct introduction to a list of related items (which are then often punctuated – separated – with semi-colons); the colon should not be followed by a dash. And to end this brief review of punctuation marks: the exclamation mark is one to be used extremely sparingly. (It is often the sign of an amateur writer unable to attract attention by words alone. Ration yourself to one 'screamer' per month.)

More 'stylistics'

An efficient, transparent, writing style entails more than can be classified as brevity and clarity though. The non-fiction author's writing should as far as possible:

● be in the active, rather than the passive voice
● be free from jargon, particularly in the 'technical' type of book and
● *flow* smoothly

It is more lively, more direct, to write, 'Gordon Wells wrote this book,' (or, 'I write this book,' but beware too many Is) than to write, 'This book was written by Gordon Wells'. The first is a statement in the active voice, the latter, in the passive voice. Wherever possible, be positive: use the active voice, rather than the passive.

Be careful using jargon. But one person's jargon is often another's everyday technical language. It is wrong to condemn outright the use of jargon; *in the right place* jargon is the right thing to use. Generally, though, at least in introductory level non-fiction books, avoid the use of jargon if at all possible.

It may sometimes, though, be useful for the reader to be made aware of the trade, hobby or profession's 'in words'. If it is necessary to introduce jargon into your non-fiction book (inevitably of the 'technical' type) – be sure to explain its meaning when first used. Use of *unintelligible* jargon is a sure sign of an author's incompetence.

The flow of your writing is one of the things that makes or mars an 'easy read'. The earlier recommendations of short sentences and short paragraphs could – if slavishly adhered to, ignoring the qualifying advice that lengths be varied – produce jumpy prose. A cobbled street rather than a smooth-surfaced highway. But the author can do more to improve the flow than just varying the lengths; otherwise disjointed paragraphs can be linked with just a few words.

Paragraph links remind the reader of where he/she has come from, and show how one paragraph follows from the thoughts of the one before.

There are many phrases that can be used to link paragraphs back to their predecessors; useful ones include:

There are other ways . . .

Similarly, . . .
That was not the only . . .
Not only does . . . but . . .
Therefore . . .
It follows that . . .

And there are always the ever-useful opening words which the old-time 'rules' said should never be used to start sentences or paragraphs:

And . . .
But . . .

The content of the writing

Leaving matters of style aside, let's look now at what you will write and how to get it started. First, some general points:

● Try to start the book, and each chapter, with a bang. Try to think up a good 'hook' – something to get the reader reading.

- In 'technical' type non-fiction books, it is often useful to start a chapter or chapter-section, by listing (eg. as 'bullet points' – like this, only briefer) several points that are to be made thereafter – and then expand on each in turn. Once the points are listed, it becomes easier to write about them – and the reader knows what to expect. This approach would not be suitable for a 'storyline' type of book, but a free-flowing introductory paragraph will serve the same purpose.
- Appeal to the reader's self-interest. Recommend specific courses of action – but mention the alternatives too.
- Illustrate your writing – not just with 'pictures', but with examples and relevant anecdotes too. Make your words mean something to the reader: it is often clearer to say eg. a lamp-standard is as high as a two-storey house, rather than (or as well as) giving its exact measurement. (Fiction writers are often advised to 'Show, don't tell'. This is good advice for the non-fiction author too.)

Many non-fiction books – of both 'technical' and 'storyline' types – are improved by the inclusion of 'real' illustrations. The non-fiction author should, whilst writing, always keep in mind the possibility of an illustration. (The preparation and presentation of illustrations are dealt with in the next chapter.) While writing though, it is important to select, visualise or roughly draw appropriate illustrations – and mention them in the text. The reference could be something like, 'Figure 0.0 shows King Hubert in his ceremonial wedding robes,' or just, 'For flow chart, *see* Figure 0.0'.

Make sure that the advice or information given in the text is the same as that shown in the illustration. That sounds like unnecessary advice – but it's easy to get it wrong, working on illustrations and text at different times. And remember, all illustrations need captions.

Photographs, reproductions of paintings, line-drawings and flow-charts are not the only 'illustrations' that can make a non-fiction book more useful. The 'technical' type of non-fiction book is often improved by tables of factual (usually numerical) information; the 'storyline' non-fiction book often includes extensive quotations.

Tables, unless no more than three or four lines in depth, should be treated just like a pictorial or diagrammatic illustration. That is, they should not be *included* in the text, but kept separate, numbered, captioned and merely referred to. (If included within the text, tables can spread across two part-pages – which looks awful.)

Quotations of up to about 50 words are usually included in the text itself, indicated merely by quote marks. Longer quotations (extracts) should not be separated in the same way as illustrations, but included in the run of the text. They should be clearly introduced and, where appropriate, their source mentioned. (When preparing the final type-script though, they should preferably be inset, sidelined and separated by a blank line above and below. The copy editor – *see* Chapter 9 – will also welcome a marginal note that it is a quotation.)

One important aspect of including quotations in your book to remember, is the need to get permission to quote. Without permission, *any* quotation can be an infringement of copyright. Your publisher will probably be able to suggest an acceptable form of words for release of copyright for quotations. The publisher will also advise you whether or not he is prepared to pay for quotations and specify an overall, limiting figure. Some authors/publishers will demand significant fees for sizeable quotations. (Remember too that you will need permission to reproduce other people's illustrations – for further advice on this, again, *see* next chapter.)

Authors of the more academic non-fiction books – both 'technical' and storyline' types – often wish to include 'on-page' footnotes. As far as possible – and totally in books for a general readership – resist this desire.

Publishers particularly dislike 'on-page' footnotes: they're difficult – and expensive. Chapter- or book-end notes are more acceptable to publishers – but many readers dislike them too, so you should still avoid using them if possible. Better, absorb the footnote content into the main text.

A final technical point about the writing content – how to write numbers. Most people, more-or-less without thinking, will write 'There are two alternatives . . .' rather than 'There are 2 alternatives . . .' Similarly, few would write 'There are one-hundred-and-thirty-four spaces in . . .' rather than 'There are 134 spaces in . . .' But where does the changeover from words to numerals come? This is decided by convention – and different publishers' house styes. One convention is to use words up to ten and numbers thereafter; another recommends spelling out all single-word numbers – that is, one to twenty – and use figures for the hyphenated double-word numbers from twenty-one onwards. Choose a convention and stick to it; consistency is what's important. And avoid starting a sentence with figures – rearrange the words.

Check, rewrite, polish

Working through your chapters, synopsis-item by synopsis-item, you'll eventually discover that you've finished the book. Well – not actually. You've only finished the first draft. There's a lot more to do yet.

First, though, heave a sigh of relief; you have at least broken the back of the book; you've got all your thoughts down on paper. You've written a book. Take a few days' rest from writing: it'll do you good. You'll come back to 'your baby' able to view it more dispassionately.

Now we come to the really hard work of authorship – converting your first draft into a readable, publishable, saleable book.

Start at the beginning – where else? – and read right through your first draft, from beginning to end. In this first full read, try not to make any style corrections: just get the *feel* of the book. Reassure yourself that it is still the book you wanted/intended/started/agreed to write. Watch out for unintentional repetitions (particularly if the two versions don't quite agree) – and more importantly, for omissions. Make notes of the omissions and repetitions; you've got to do something about them. Do it now – write the extra section to fill the gap, and after careful thought, delete one of the repeated sections. Scissors-and-paste these amendments into your first-draft typescript.

Now go back to the beginning of the book and start again, chapter by chapter, in detail. I have already mentioned the advantages of reading your written work aloud; it is one of the best methods of checking a draft. Reading aloud identifies the pomposities and the confused thinking; if you find it difficult or uncomfortable to read a particular section aloud, it probably needs rewriting. If you stumble over a long word – change it. Check all facts, figures and dates too.

At the same time, look carefully at the appearance of the paragraphs. Are some too long? Are there too many of the same length? Does that extra-long paragraph really only contain one thought? It'll almost certainly be better if you split it.

Watch out, too, for over-long sentences. Read them carefully: then either accept them (as a one-off over the average) or split them.

As you read, ask yourself whether it's an 'easy read'. If it's not, you may lose your reader. As you read, watch for clumsy phrasing – and improve it. As you read, check for over-use of favourite words or phrases; check whether you have repeated any words too close to each other. If you can find correct alternatives, change them. Polish your writing – put a shine on it. And – check your spelling.

Editing others' contributions

As mentioned earlier, some academic 'technical' type non-fiction books are written by several contributors, the whole being pulled together by an editor. If that is your role, be prepared to exercise considerable tact – some people will fight tooth and nail to preserve a semi-colon or pet word – and much technical and literary skill. You have to:

● Establish a degree of CONTINUITY throughout the whole book. This is perhaps best done by discussing and agreeing detailed chapter synopses before work starts. Beware of – and adjudicate on – differing interpretations of supposed 'facts'.
● Establish an APPEARANCE of uniformity throughout the book. Establish a standard approach to the hierarchy and frequency of headings (*see* Chapter 5) and to the treatment of tables, illustrations, etc.
● Check all contributions for READABILITY. Rewrite with tact and sensitivity for the author's feelings – and then obtain approval for changes. Edit out all gobbledegook and inappropriate jargon.
● Check and correct the word choice, spelling and punctuation.
● Ensure that the publisher's delivery timetable is adhered to. This is a near impossible and thankless task. But it's important to try.

It's often easier to write the whole darn thing yourself! (That's the one exclamation mark for this book.) Good luck.

7

ILLUSTRATING THE BOOK

'What is the use of a book,' thought Alice, 'without pictures . . . ?'

Lewis Carroll

Illustrations are important. Just about every non-fiction book – 'technical' and 'storyline' alike – is improved by good illustrations. They are the first thing people look at when they flip through the pages of a book. They may tip the balance in favour of a sale.

But illustrations cost money and take up space. An American newspaper magnate once said that one good picture was worth a thousand words of print. No doubt that's true – as long as it's a good picture and earns its space. Some illustrations can cost more than the words they might replace. The selection or design of illustrations for a non-fiction book – for adults, if not for children – is often a process of excluding the interesting in favour of the essential.

The functions of illustrations in a non-fiction book are, in random order of importance:

● to help the reader to visualise something more easily than by reading a description or trying to absorb columns of figures; to make the description 'come alive'.
● to portray a process where, for instance, it would be difficult to describe the concurrence of several activities as clearly as they could be drawn – for example in a flow chart.
● to break up the text – to relieve the areas of grey print.
● to make the book's pages look more attractive.

Illustrations are particularly important in non-fiction books for children; 'jokey' illustrations are sometimes included in relatively serious books – to brighten up the overall *feel*.

Every illustration – in 'technical' or 'storyline' books, in adult or children's books – should enhance the text, not merely duplicate an already adequate description. An illustration should always be informative, if only in clarifying the text.

Types of illustration

To the writer and to the reader, the illustrations in a book are either 'pictures' or 'diagrams' – a classification based solely on appearance; in some 'technical' type books, there are also 'words in boxes' – flow charts – that are treated as diagrammatic illustrations. (Figure 4.1 is an example.) 'Storyline' type non-fiction books will of course seldom use anything other than pictorial illustrations.

To the printer, black and white illustrations are either *half-tone* or *line*. This classification is based on the tonal content of the illustration rather than on its appearance. And although most half-tone illustrations are pictorial and most diagrammatic (etc.) illustrations are line drawings, there is no inevitable link between the writer's or reader's classification and the printer's.

Any illustration that contains an area of continuous (but variable depth) tone is treated as half-tone – which is a photographic process.

Line illustrations are pictures made up exclusively of lines, dots and solid black areas. Line illustrations are easy (and cheap) to incorporate in any book. Even today, though, when printing techniques make it possible to incorporate words, pictures and diagrams on all of a book's pages – as is common in many children's non-fiction books – it is still more usual (and cheaper) for quality photographic illustrations in a basically text-oriented book to be grouped on separate, glossy-paper pages.

Agree with your publisher – in advance – whether you can include line drawings and/or half-tone illustrations in your book.

Despite the apparent preponderance of colour illustration in some books – particularly coffee-table books and those for children –

colour is still expensive. A non-fiction author who is committed to providing the illustrations for a book should not assume that colour pictures will automatically be acceptable; you MUST check with your publisher before you start collecting together a batch of colour illustrations. (And the matter of who provides the illustrations is an important distinction: many children's non-fiction publishers will allow, in their pre-commissioning calculations, for colour illustrations – and produce them themselves.)

It is important for the non-fiction author to know who is to provide – and pay for – the illustrations for the book. The likely alternatives are outlined in the table [opposite].

If your publisher wants, or agrees to you providing, colour illustrations for your non-fiction book, be prepared to produce transparencies rather than colour prints. (35 mm slides may not be acceptable, unless of exceptional quality; larger sized, more expensive transparencies will usually be required.)

Preparing line illustrations

A drawing prepared for any other purpose is unlikely to be suitable for use as a book illustration. Book illustrations should be purpose-made. They should be:

● simple and uncluttered – too much detail can confuse the reader
● well labelled, yet not excessively (maximum 25 words of labelling)
● clear – there should be no doubt of the illustration's purpose

The form in which you produce line drawings should be a matter for agreement between you and the publisher. The alternatives are finished (unlettered) drawings or rough sketches. The rough sketches (roughs) should not be *too* rough though. Ideally, they will be correct in every detail and to the correct size – but perhaps only in pencil. The publisher's draughtsman will prefer being able merely to trace – in ink, with the right weight of line – directly from the roughs. (How you present your drawings will affect the publisher's costs – and may just tip the balance of a book's commercial acceptability.)

WHO PROVIDES THE ILLUSTRATIONS?

ILLUSTRATION TYPE	SOURCE/PROVIDER
'Storyline' type books Almost exclusively half-tone, pictorial illustrations, usually black and white photographs or photographic reproductions of paintings, etc.	Author selects pictures - from own sources and/or from picture library/agencies - committing the publisher to paying reproduction fees, usually against an 'illustration budget' set by the publisher
'Technical' type books Some half-tone, pictorial illustrations, usually black and white photographs	As for 'storyline' type books, possibly without any payment by the publisher
Usually mostly line drawings, including diagrams, flow charts, graphs, working drawings, maps, etc.	Ideally, author provides finished black and white drawings - but this is often not possible (few authors are artists too). Best alternative is for the author to provide 'roughs' - rough, but true-to-scale, sketches - for publisher's artist to redraw
Children's non-fiction books Frequently pictorial line drawings, usually in colour, sometimes humorous	Virtually always drawn by publisher's staff/commissioned artist. Author is encouraged - sometimes required - to offer suggestions, or to provide detailed artist's briefing
Often colour photographs	Author may be encouraged or required to locate/identify sources for photographs

Illustrations – whether in line or half-tone – can be either upright ('portrait') or horizontal ('landscape'). It is always distracting for a reader to have to rotate the book to study a 'landscape' illustration that fills a page. Wherever possible therefore, avoid horizontal illustrations that cannot be accommodated within the width of the page's type area.

Many books (specifically those produced to the popular metric *Demy octavo* 138 mm x 216 mm page size) have a type area of 100 mm width and about 160 to 170 mm depth (depending on whether a running head is used). Line illustrations should preferably be drawn larger than the intended finished size – the reduction hides minor blemishes. And, because whole batches of drawings are usually reduced together, it is important that drawings are prepared for standard degrees of reduction. The most common reduction factors are 50 and 67 per cent – requiring originals to be twice or one-and-a-half times print size. 'Originals' – whether finished or roughs – should therefore be drawn within 200 mm x about 300 mm or 150 mm x about 220 mm boundaries – these depths being reduced to accommodate the captions. (Coincidentally, the 200 mm x 300 mm size is close to that of a sheet of A4 paper – which I use for all line drawings and their equivalent. *See* page 61 for an example.)

Because of the reduction process, not only does the overall drawing need to be 'larger than life', but so too do the lines with which it is drawn. Two or three line thicknesses (*weights*) will usually suffice. These are:

At print size		At original size:	
		for 50% reduction	for 67% reduction
light	0.12 mm	0.25 mm	0.2 mm
normal	0.3 mm	0.6 mm	0.4 mm
heavy	0.4 mm	0.8 mm	0.6 mm

There are a number of inexpensive liquid ink, 0.5 and 0.7 mm metal point, high-tech pens now available which will be perfectly adequate for an author's occasional use. (There are also proper draughting pens which could be a sensible purchase for an author producing a large number of line drawings.) I've also successfully produced line drawings using a brand-new nylon-tipped pen. The ink must, in all cases, be good, strong, smooth-flowing and *black*.

You will be extremely wise, even if you are producing finished line drawings, to arrange for the publisher to have the in-picture lettering added. Lettering for print is extremely difficult to do well; don't try it.

Draw your illustrations (finished or roughs) on good quality A4 paper – no publisher has yet objected to my use of 80 gsm typing paper. (An added advantage of using A4 paper is that the illustrations can then be packed with the typescript – *see* next chapter.) If providing roughs, include all necessary lettering – in capital letters to avoid misinterpretation – on the drawing. If providing finished drawings but without lettering, my own preferred practice is to provide a pristine original plus a photocopy with the lettering added, again in capitals. The other approach is lightly to pencil in the lettering on the original. (It is also wise to retain a photocopy of each illustration for your own records.)

Half-tone illustrations

As already suggested, most half-tone illustrations in non-fiction books will be photographs. And non-photographs are usually best photographed anyway. But it is not necessary for the non-fiction author to take the photographs – indeed, if not an expert photographer, it may well be better not.

Photographs for use in non-fiction books should be:

- black and white prints – unless it has been specifically agreed in advance with the publisher that colour is acceptable
- needle-sharp – poor focusing will detract from the whole book
- printed on glossy rather than matt paper
- well-contrasted – without being 'soot and whitewash'
- larger than print size – 200 mm x 150 mm is a good standard (and will be ideal for 50 per cent reduction – *see* above – to give a half-page horizontal picture)
- full of the subject – ie. the subject fills the picture
- unmounted – but don't try to separate from an existing mount

It will nearly always be the author's responsibility to identify and locate suitable photographs for use in the book. Unless taken by the author, the copyright of nearly all photographs belongs to someone else – and reproduction has to be paid for. Other than commissioned purpose-made photographs you will be able to get photographs from museums, art galleries, photographic agencies, picture libraries and – sometimes for free reproduction for publicity benefits – from commercial firms and government departments. Be careful though: a museum, art gallery, etc. may sell you a picture of an exhibit; the fact that you have bought the picture does not give you the right to repro-duce it in your book; for that you will have to pay a much larger reproduction fee. Don't pay this at the time of purchase. Ask what the fee will be – for payment when the final selection has been made.

Ideally, you will have agreed with the publisher a budget – the amount that the publisher will pay in reproduction fees – for photographs; you will also need to get written reproduction releases for each photograph.

Presentation of illustrations

The most important point about presentation of illustrations is – don't incorporate them into the typescript. Illustrations should be carefully numbered – light soft-pencilled numbers on the back of photographs, or on the front of line drawings (in the corner). You should usually – unless specifically advised otherwise by your publisher – number all illustrations, irrespective of type, consecutively by chapter. Thus: Fig 1.1, Fig 1.2, Fig 1.3, Fig 2.1, Fig 3.1 . . . etc.

You will sometimes want to have additional artwork done on a photograph – something to be masked out perhaps. Indicate this by sticking a sheet of thin (preferably translucent) paper to the back of the print and folding it over the front; mark artwork requirements, again, in soft pencil, on the overlay – in the appropriate place. If you press too hard you could damage the underlying photograph.

Finished drawings, roughs and photographs should then be grouped together, in order, separate from the typescript for delivery to the publisher. It's a good idea to interleave photographs with thin (eg. Bank) paper for protection. You should pack the illustrations in a separate envelope or wallet from the typescript and – sensibly – enclose a list of what's there. Captions – *see* below – should be packed with the typescript; but an extra copy of the caption list makes a good list of 'illustrations enclosed'.

Artist's briefs – for children's books

As already mentioned, for some children's non-fiction books, the author may be expected to provide suggestions, reference material, and helpful information/advice for the artist: the artist's brief. As well as photocopies of reference material, this will usually consist of a description of the illustration you envisage. There are few rights and wrongs about such briefs – indeed, there are artists who prefer only minimal briefs. But if you want the book to turn out as you have visualised it, offer a helpful brief. It need only be fairly casual – 'I suggest . . .' or 'Some sort of . . . might be a good idea here'.

In the dinosaur book that I wrote for young children, the brief for a 2-page spread describing the Cretaceous Period was:

> Illustration page 30-31: A sparse woodland scene with distant pine-like trees and nearer ferns, with *triceratops* dinosaurs feeding on the lower ferns. The scene is split by a small stream leading out to the visible sea – over and towards which a *pteranodon* is diving.

I provided photocopied drawings of the *triceratops* and the *pteranodon* for other pages in the book; I provided a photocopied picture of typical scenery too. The resultant book-page looked good – and close enough to my concept.

Captions

Captions have already been mentioned. Every illustration –

photograph, diagram, flow chart, table, etc. – in a non-fiction book requires a caption. (Or sometimes merely a title – like the table in this chapter.) After the illustration itself, the caption is often the next thing a potential purchaser notices in the book. The captions are much read. It is important to get them right.

A caption should state clearly and unambiguously what the illustration is of. It is not usually the place for adding further information that should more appropriately be in the main text. At the same time, the caption should be 'self-contained'. Where appropriate, bear in mind the time-honoured journalists' questions: Who? What? Why? Where? When? and How? Captions should not be too long: 25 words is a good maximum length to aim at.

Type all the captions, in order, in list format, numbered to correspond with the illustrations. As for all other parts of the typescript (*see* next chapter), the captions should be typed in double spacing on A4 paper. They should be packed and delivered with, but separate from, the typescript. (Possibly, in a separate envelope within the overall wallet.)

8

PREPARING THE TYPESCRIPT

The place for originality is in your writing – not in preparing the final typescript. There is – basically – just one acceptable way in which to present your work to your publisher; there is no room here for innovation. (The reason for that qualifying 'basically' is because more publishers are beginning to welcome manuscripts on computer disk – in addition to the 'usual' typescript.) You must present your work in the form that is most convenient for the publisher and the printer.

Before you start preparing the final typescript version, though, stop and think. No matter how you have been committing your words to paper – in handwriting, on a typewriter or via the word processor screen – now is your last realistic chance to check on what you've written. Reread your last, finished draft in its entirety: not paragraph by paragraph as you did when polishing, nor even chapter by chapter, but straight through. Lock yourself away one evening and read it right through as you would a novel.

Check for consistency. Did you say, in Chapter 1, something like '. . . as explained more fully in Chapter 0'? And did you pick this up in the later chapter? If not, do something about it: take out the initial allusion or insert the later explanation – and correct the missing chapter number. Read the finished draft as one coming new to the book. Does it really grab you? Ignoring false modesty, it should make you say to yourself, 'That's good; I like it; I'd buy this'.

You will sometimes wish to show the completed book manuscript – or just part – to someone else before final submission: a colleague or expert to check specific facts; or a friend perhaps to check that it reads easily. Be careful, though, the book is yours: welcome factual corrections but add lots of salt to opinions. (Remember: a camel was just a horse – until it got 'done over' by a committee.)

Not only must the draft be ready for final typing, so must everything else. When you deliver the typescript to the publisher he wants it all in one batch: main text, illustrations, captions, preliminary pages (*see* below), appendices, bibliographies.

If you deliver the whole package short of one chapter or the illustrations – you might just as well not bother. The typescript will just have to sit and wait until the missing part arrives; and sections of incomplete sedentary typescripts have been known to go a-wandering.

Delivery of an incomplete typescript makes the publisher more than usually frustrated; his opinion of you will drop a notch or three. And if delivery of the missing part is after the deadline, this may prejudice the whole production timetable.

So, the form of presentation ...

Typescript layout

There are no two ways about it – book manuscripts *must* be typescripts. A handwritten manuscript just won't get looked at. (The words – manuscript and typescript – are commonly interchangeable.) One of the most important things to remember throughout the preparation of the typescript is, above all, to:

BE CONSISTENT – IN SPELLING AND LAYOUT

The manuscript can be typed on a typewriter or by a word processor's printer; it matters not which. It can be in pica or elite typescript or it can be in immaculate computer-generated print-like characters: it doesn't matter. (If you do use print-like characters, just don't make them too small – about the same size as typescript is fine.) The word processor's printer can be a laser printer, an ink-jet printer, a daisy-wheel printer or a dot-matrix printer – as long as the latter doesn't produce 'dotty' characters. (A 24-pin dot-matrix printer is fine; a 9-pin machine in 'ordinary, single-pass' mode is not.)

It is far, far better for any writer to do his or her own typing. Employing someone to type a book manuscript for you will cost a small fortune. Not only that – if you do your own typing, you have this final opportunity to correct last-minute errors.

The whole book manuscript must be typed on one side only of good quality A4 (297 x 210 mm) paper; 80 gsm (grammes per square metre) paper is about the right weight. The typing must be double-spaced throughout – and for the avoidance of doubt, this means type a line, miss a whole (not half-space) line space. Do not type quotations or inset material in single-spaced – everything must be double-spaced.

Allow good large margins all round: about 40-50 mm on the left side and 25 mm at top, bottom and right side. These margins are needed for editors' and printers' instructions and notes. Figure 9.1 (on page 106) serves two purposes: it shows a page of typical well set out typescript and the copy editor's corrections and printer's instructions thereon.

Keep the lines of typescript as near as possible the same length throughout; work to a constant number of lines per typed page too. If your word processor program or typewriter will let you produce 'right-justified' typescript – that is, with a straightened-out right edge – switch this facility off and leave the right edge ragged. Machines right-justify by inserting extra gaps between words – and the typesetter can't tell whether they are author-required or machine-added spaces. Keep it simple and don't do it.) Also avoid hyphenating words in order to squeeze them in at line-ends – these 'soft' hyphens, too, can confuse the typesetter.

Start each chapter on a fresh page. Type the chapter number a few lines down the page and its title a few lines below that; start the text a further few lines down. If you are using within-chapter headings, leave at least one line space above and below them.

I recommend that you type both chapter titles and headings in lower case letters, starting flush at the left margin; if the publisher wants to use capital letters and/or centred titles or headings, this is a simple correction – easier than 'undoing' capitals. And don't underline the chapter titles or headings: mark their 'weight' in the left margin, in pencil – [Chap] for chapter title, [A] for 'first-level' headings and, if you must, [B] for 'second-level' headings. (*See* also Chapter 5 for the hierarchy of headings.)

At the beginning of each chapter, and beneath each heading, don't indent the paragraph start; begin it flush with the left margin. Indent the start of all other paragraphs by a consistent number of spaces – a five-space indent is common practice. Do not leave a blank line between paragraphs. Do not underline anything that is not to be printed in italics: reserve italics for strange or foreign words, book and magazine titles . . . and occasional emphasis. (Beginning authors are prone to over-use of italics. So am I, but I take out my excess underlining at the polishing stage.) Above all – be consistent.

If yours is a 'technical' type non-fiction book you may wish to include the occasional table and/or, more often, 'bullet-point' lists – to which we have already referred.

Only small – three-four line – tables may be included in the text; treat all others as illustrations and type them on separate sheets – complete with title or caption – and, as with any other illustration, refer to them in the text. (*See* also Chapter 6.) Avoid using vertical lines to separate columns in a table: vertical lines are expensive – space looks better.

Type your 'bullet-point' lists using a lower-case O for the bullet; it is not necessary to go through your typescript inking these in. Type the bullet at the left margin, without an indent; leave a couple of spaces between bullet and start of text; range text within the list below the first word, not below the bullet. (That is, the bullet itself is a reversed-indent.)

All the typescript pages must, of course, be numbered. The preferred location for the page number is at the top right corner. Typescript pages should be numbered straight through the whole text. (Rather than, as might be appropriate in some academic papers or management reports, chapter by chapter.) It is useful/helpful for the numbering also to include some identification; my own practice is to type a key-word from the book's title, my name and the page number – thus, 'Non-fiction/Wells/00'. Of course, a word processor will do this automatically: merely set up a 'header'.

The importance of consistency has already been mentioned. So far, mainly matters of typing layout have been considered. But consistency in word-use, spelling and punctuation is also of paramount importance.

Points to watch out for include:

● where there are alternative ways of naming or describing something, standardising on one – or, if you must use an alternative, ensure that this is made abundantly clear. And . . . are you going to write 'photo-copy' or 'photocopy', 'full stop' or 'full-stop'? Decide, one way or the other, and stick to it.

- the modern preference for the use of -ise spelling rather than -ize.
- uses of initial capital letters: generally use capitals sparingly – amateur writers are prone to over-use capitals. (Use 'a duke' rather than 'a Duke' – but when specific, use 'the Duke of Norfolk'.
- use of per cent: use separate words (not percent) and precede by figures (not words). Except in tables, avoid the abbreviated % form.
- use of punctuation: omit full stops within groups of initials and after abbreviations; thus WHO, MP, Mr, Ms, Lt-Col Smith. When first using an uncommon abbreviation, spell it out in full, followed by the abbreviation in parenthesis, or vice versa if the abbreviation is the favoured form – such as computer RAM (Random Access Memory).
- use of quotation marks: modern practice is to use single quote marks for speech or quotations, reserving double quote marks for secondary use, ie. quotations within quotations.

Most publishers have their own preferred *house style*. This will usually include most of the above, which are commonly agreed; they will often have other idiosyncrasies of their own. In the absence of specific house style guidance from 'your' publisher, consult *The Oxford Writers' Dictionary* (OUP) and also ensure that, when in doubt, your manuscript is internally consistent.

Some publishers extend the concept of house style (which usually deals only with things like spelling and punctuation) to the specific layout of the typescript. These requirements are normally straightforward: characters per line of typescript, number of lines per page, line-spaces above and below headings, etc. Comply with such specifications if at all possible – it makes life easier for the publisher. Such requirements are but a small step along the path towards supplying complete manuscripts on computer disk for easier editing and typesetting (*see* below).

Logistics

Your final typescript should *look* good. The publisher may be committed to the book but he will still prefer to work on a typescript that is clear and easily read.

Fit a new ribbon in your typewriter or computer printer: if you use a part-worn one, the print will become too faint before the typescript is complete. If you're using a typewriter, check the typefaces too, for cleanliness. (This is the time for you to make a good impression.)

The paper on which the book manuscript is typed should be white, A4 sized and of good quality: I use 80 gsm (grammes per square metre) copier paper for all purposes. (If you are using type-writer and carbon paper, the use of bank paper for other than the top copy will enhance the copy-quality; remember to change the carbon paper frequently too.) Once the three full sets (top copy and one more for the publisher, one set for your own retention) of typescript are complete, separate them out and file your set in a binder. Read carefully through your set: check for missing lines, spelling errors, missing cross-references . . . and of course, any major omissions.

No matter how carefully you checked before final typing/printing, it is inevitable that one or two errors will have crept in. If these are merely the odd typo, correct the typescript pages in ink; if there are major corrections to be made, retype one or more pages.

If there are major omissions type these on fresh sheets and insert them in the numbered pages: mark the foot of the last correct sheet (001) '001a follows'; number the new pages 001a, 001b, etc.; at the foot of the last added sheet, type '002 follows' and at the top right of page 002 add the words 'follows page 001c'. In other words, make it clear that there are added pages. If you need to delete existing typescript – either because it's wrongly included or to accommodate additional material – mark the deletion clearly with a Z-shaped line, in ink.

Never cut typescript pages in two or glue added material on a page so that it either overlaps required text, or sticks out to the side. Whether cut or added to, make up to full A4-sized sheets – with a Z-shaped line through any unused space.

If you are using a word processor, you should probably reprint a whole chapter to accommodate insertions or deletions. Adjust the page numbering at the end of the reprinted chapter as explained above.

Once all copies of the typescript are, as far as you now know, complete and correct, go through them all and, in the left margin, in pencil, mark the preferred locations for illustrations, tables, etc. Write [Fig 1.1] or [Table 23] or . . . and rely on the printer (and/or the book designer) to bring them into the book as close as possible to that. (You will already have marked the 'weight' of the headings – [Chap], [A], etc.)

Prelims and end-matter

While a novel seldom has much more in it than the text itself, this is not the case with a non-fiction book. Look at the non-fiction books on your own bookshelves: there are contents pages, there may be appendices, occasionally bibliographies – and always, an index. The peripheral pages at the front of the book are called preliminary pages – or more often *prelims*; the 'extra' pages at the end are known as *end-matter*. Both prelims and end-matter are important parts of a non-fiction book – and the non-fiction author has to provide at least some of them.

The first few preliminary pages in a non-fiction book are standard; usually numbered in small roman figures, they should be:

page (i)   *Half-title*. Always a right-hand page (recto). It contains only the book title.

page (ii) *Half-title verso*. The reverse (verso) of the half-title and thus always a left-hand page. Here, subject to the agreement of your publisher, might be listed other books you have written – or books by other writers in the same series.

page (iii) *Title-page*. Always a right-hand page. It carries the book's full title, with subtitle, if any; the author's name (with academic qualifications – if relevant); and the publisher's imprint/logo, or his name and abbreviated address.

page (iv) *Title-page verso*. The reverse of the title-page and thus always a left-hand page. This page is used for legal and bibliographical requirements. Its contents include the publisher's name and address, the copyright notice and author's moral right assertion, the book's publishing history, the ISBN and the printer's name. If space is short, brief dedications or acknowledgements may be accommodated on the title-verso. (If spare space is available, a dedication is given a right-hand page of its own, with a blank verso.

page (v) *Contents*. Conventionally, these begin on a right-hand page. Details of the contents page details are outlined below.

From the contents page onward, the prelims vary from book to book. You should discuss any special requirements – a dedication, a list of illustrations or a preface (but such extras are seldom appropriate in other than the more heavyweight titles) – with your publisher.

Your publisher will probably welcome being provided with typed draft prelims for all of the above; it is essential that you provide the title-page and the contents page. (Some authors like to specify the book's total wordage on the title page.)

The contents page is an important part of every non-fiction book: it is 'the native guide to the territory'; it is the reader's first resort when searching for coverage of a particular aspect. It should be prepared from the typescript and be an exact replication of at least the chapter titles and the titles of the end-matter. For most 'technical' type non-fiction books, which have in-chapter headings, the contents page is improved by including the headings too – as in this book, page (v). Again, these must be precisely as in the typescript.

Some authors of 'storyline' type non-fiction books like to include similar expansions of the chapter contents even though they don't use headings in the text. This is often a good idea but is a matter for agreement with the publisher. It will help the editor if you include on the contents page, in pencil, the typescript page numbers of chapter starts. But do add a pencil note to the effect that they are typescript page numbers only; later, they will need to be corrected to book pages.

A non-fiction book's end matter is less standardised than are the prelims. It may consist of some or all of the following: appendices, endnotes (replacing the unpopular footnotes), bibliography (or the more 'friendly-sounding' reading list), and, last but not least, the index.

There are conventions for the preparation of the bibliography and of references in the endnotes. In the bibliography, refer to books by, in order: author's name, book title (underlined for italics, not in quotes, plus edition number, where relevant), and the publisher's name in parenthesis. (In the more formal bibliographies, publisher's location and date are also quoted, within the brackets.) Books should be listed alphabetically by author; in formal bibliographies the author's name is written surname first; in less formal reading lists, as in this book, the author's name is often shown conventionally. An author's first name is preferred to initials. In endnotes, where a book is referred to, the author's name is always written conventionally. All end-matter page numbers should follow on from the numbering of the main text.

Prelims and end-matter should all – in common with the rest of the typescript – be typed double-spaced. With the exception of the index, they should all be delivered with the main text.

(My own practice is also to deliver a first draft of the index, based on typescript page numbers – which fact I make very clear – together with the rest of the material. This gives the publisher an indication of the length of the index and allows space to be allocated to it. *See* below for further advice on preparing the index.)

Delivery to the publisher

Your typescript is at last complete. All the pages are numbered consecutively, with prelims numbered in a separate sequence. You have the copies separated out: 'top' copy possibly plus one for the publisher, your own file copy – and, if you have an agent (*see* Chapter 10), an extra copy for her too. All the illustrations are ready – either as roughs or finished drawings – and, where appropriate, you have obtained photocopies for your own files. Captions are ready. Any necessary copyright approvals have been granted and release documents are on your files. Everything is ready.

Don't put the top copy typescript in a fancy binder, don't staple pages together by chapter, don't punch a hole in the corner and insert a Treasury tag. Just bundle everything up (prelims, main text, end-matter, illustrations), put an elastic band around it and put it in a cardboard wallet – or the box the typing paper came in. Do the same with the publisher's second set. Stick a identifying label on the wallet or box saying, in large letters, something like: HOW TO WRITE NON-FICTION BOOKS – Gordon Wells – 'Top'/'Second' copy.

My own custom is also to provide a single, close-typed page to act as something like an invoice or packing slip – a list of what I am sending. It says something like:

HOW TO WRITE NON-FICTION BOOKS   Gordon Wells

I enclose

- 6 sheets of prelims, numbered (i) to (vi)
- 376 sheets of main text (in 23 chapters – 95,000 words) and end-matter
- 4 sheets of DRAFT index, numbered I-a to I-d (NB: manu-script-folio numbers only. Provided merely to indicate space needed)

- 2 sheets of captions for illustrations

- 10 sheets of illustrations (in separate envelope, original only)

NOTES

(Here I include particular points to which editorial attention might be needed – such as ensuring an over-sized word-illustration is set in a smaller type than usual, in order to fit onto a single page. I also explain the marginal notes on the heading hierarchy.)

Whenever possible, I prefer to deliver the whole typescript by hand. Delivery will of course be on or before your deadline. You agreed to work to this date; if you were unlikely to meet the deadline – even by working nights – you should long ago have forewarned the   publisher and agreed a revised delivery date. Depending on my   relationship with my editor, I may either telephone or write to warn of delivery. Unless this produces an invitation to call in, I merely deliver the

the package to the publisher's reception desk and walk away. At least I know that my baby has arrived safely. Everything that needs saying should be in the 'packing list/invoice' or in an earlier letter.

If I didn't use a word processor – from which a further copy is only a key-stroke away – and delivery by post were unavoidable, I would post original and copy typescripts in two separate packages, one by registered post. And I always ask the publisher to acknowledge receipt, supplying him with a stamped addressed envelope for the purpose.

Delivery on computer disk

If you have a word processor, more and more publishers will welcome your also providing them with a floppy disk containing the book manuscript as COPIES (never the originals) of your computer files. If you use one of the better known, widely used word processor programs (WordPerfect, Word, WordStar, etc.) you may be able to supply 'ordinary' word processor files; you must check this with your publisher.

If you use a less well-known program – as I do – then most publishers are happy with what are known as ASCII files (ASCII = American Standard Code for Information Interchange). ASCII files contain the complete text but none of the subsidiary text controls – indents, underlining, etc. And each line of text in an ASCII file is self-contained – it will not word-wrap (run onto the next line) as a word processor program does.

Delivery on disk saves postage – particularly when mailing work abroad. But the disk alone is not enough. The publisher also needs a 'master' typescript, to assist in reading the computer file. (When I send work abroad, as ASCII files on disk, my publisher is content with a single-spaced 'master' typescript.) Make each chapter a separate, manageable, computer file rather than a single file for the whole book. And use understandable titles for the files. My files for this book are all called HNF (the book title in brief) C (for chapter) 00 (the chapter), making this file HNFC08.EXP. The EXP suffix is my program's auto-identification of an ASCII file.

Starting on the index

As already mentioned, I believe it is helpful to submit a draft index together with the rest of the book manuscript. For this, work from your 'hard' file copy of the manuscript (ie. not the computer files).

Work right through your manuscript and underline in coloured ink (for easy spotting) everything important, everything that may need to be referred back to. Where a single word or phrase best describes a description or argument, yet does not appear on the page, then write the word/phrase, in colour, at the top of the relevant page. Because of their importance, virtually every chapter title and heading should be marked for indexing; so too should check lists, illustrations, etc. In 'storyline' type non-fiction books, each mention of every significant person should usually be colour-marked for indexing.

If you don't have a computer, you must now prepare sheets of plain paper, each marked with the letters of the alphabet. (Group less-used letters – IJK, PQ, UV, XYZ – together on single sheets.) Now work through the file copy manuscript again; note each colour-marked item and its manuscript page onto the appropriate alphabetical sheet. Be sure to index it as many times as necessary: for example, 'word budget' should be noted as 'word budget' and also as 'budget, word'. When all the colour-marked items are recorded on the alphabetical sheets, there may well be twenty or so items per sheet. It is then no great task to put these in alphabetical order within each sheet. (I go through the list again and again muttering to myself, 'Ra, Ra, Ra – nothing; Rb, Rc, Rd – impossible; Re, Re, – reviewers, folio 45; Re, Re, – no more; Rf, Rg, Rh, Ri, Ri, Ri – Right justification, folio 83'. And so on. Ignore word-splits.

It is then a simple task to type out the index items and pencil in the folio numbers.

If you have a computer and a spread-sheet program, type the index items into that: the program can re-arrange them in alphabetical order.

Then transfer the alphabetical list from spread-sheet to word processor. Some word processor programs themselves include an indexing facility which may be useful. Both typed/pencilled index and spread-sheet-ordered index will need to be corrected later to reflect book pages. For details on this, *see* next chapter.

9

FROM TYPESCRIPT TO BOOK

Your complete typescript has been delivered. What does the publisher do with it?

It will go first to the commissioning or sponsoring editor for reading. Usually the commissioning editor will read it right through herself; she will also often ask someone who is a specialist in the book's subject to read it for her. The first task of editor and/or specialist reader is to check the book for accuracy, coverage of the subject, accidental omissions, interest – and understandability.

(You have been immersed in your subject, your nose pressed to the grindstone, for months, while writing your book. It is easy for an author not to notice an imperceptible falling off of understandability. And if an experienced editor or a specialist reader finds it hard to understand what you mean, what chance is there for the beginner – the target-reader? This check-reading is very much to your advantage.)

When the readers have reported to the editor, she will review their comments – decide what weight to put on them. If there are points of consequence, the readers' reports – or extracts therefrom – will often be referred to you for your consideration. The editor may ask you to rewrite one or more sections of the book. Most books will need only little rewriting and that usually just for greater clarification.

Don't be worried or upset by such requests (so long as they are not too extensive). They are not at all unusual – and, as already mentioned, usually beneficial. And even if the changes asked for are extensive, as long as you accept that they are sensible, they are worth making. Alternatively, go back to your editor and try to convince her that you're right and she and the specialist readers are wrong.

Literary pride is out of place in such a situation; if a partial rewrite will mean your book selling better – get rewriting.

At about this time, depending on the terms of your Agreement, you may be eligible for a further part of the advance against your royalties – as mentioned in Chapter 4. (And *see* also Chapter 10.) The better Agreements provide for the advance on delivery of the manuscript; some, less good (from the author's viewpoint), on acceptance.

(I have had commissioned books cancelled after delivery – not for any fault with the books, but merely from a change in publishing policy. In such cases, you would certainly retain the 'on signing' part of the advance – a good reason for seeking the largest advance possible on signing – and ought to receive the balance of the advance as compensation for non-publication.)

Money aside, the commissioning editor should by now be satisfied with the content of your manuscript. Maybe you will have rewritten a chapter. (Chapter 1 is always a tricky one to get right – I once rewrote an opening chapter three times before the publisher was satisfied.) You may have had to change the sequence of some sections or chapters or sections – or maybe it was all satisfactory without change. But whatever, it's now finally accepted.

The manuscript now passes to the copy-editor – who may be the same person, but wearing a different hat. Commissioning and copy-editors have very different roles.

Meanwhile, a second copy of your book manuscript may go to the production staff – for them to get cost estimates from printers, etc. It may also be shown to potential purchasers of foreign rights.

Copy-editing

The copy-editor is concerned with the 'quality' of your manuscript rather than its content. The copy-editor's task is to check and in some cases polish your writing; to check for consistency of style both within your writing and with the publisher's house style (already mentioned, in Chapter 8); and to prepare the typescript for despatch to the typesetters and printers.

Copy-editors are individuals, all different. Some, probably frustrated 'creative' writers, delight in making many stylistic changes to a non-fiction author's text – coming near to rewriting whole sections; others are content merely to correct the author's faults while leaving the style undisturbed. Beware the first type: against the possibility of being 'serviced' by one such, insist on sight of your edited manuscript before it is sent to the printers. You can then undo much of the harm possibly done to your work.

Most non-fiction authors have a love-hate relationship with their copy-editors. I have a rather casual writing style; when I come up against a fussy copy-editor there are sometimes problems. Against that, several of my books have been much improved by sympathetic and careful copy-editing: correcting my occasional grammatical howlers, spelling mistakes and punctuation errors.

(I tend to over-use the dash: I try to restrain myself, but some copy-editors replace far too many of them. I have learnt a lot by studying the changes copy-editors have made to other aspects of my punctuation – and having consistently mis-spelled *accommodate* throughout one book, I was extremely grateful to the copy-editor who corrected it. But one over-pedantic copy-editor expunged every 'and' and 'but' with which I had occasionally – and deliberately – started sentences in one book; this was one time when I did not see the edited typescript. Nor do I want to come across that copy-editor again.)

Criticism apart, copy-editors meet an essential need; all authors should be grateful for the skill and guidance of their copy-editors. But you cannot expect a copy-editor to be expert in your speciality; you should always check that they have not inadvertently changed the sense of your words. (Another reason for the pre-typesetting check of the edited typescript.)

The other thing that the copy-editor does is prepare the typescript for typesetting. This entails marking it with instructions for the typesetter: a good printed page layout is not necessarily the same as a well laid-out page of typescript. For example, most typists indent paragraph starts by five or ten spaces: on the printed page, it is customary to indent by about two spaces (one *em* in printing terms). Similarly, while a bullet-point list of two or three short items can look good in typescript, the copy-editor may decide that they will look better in print if run on, in one sentence.

Figure 9.1 shows a typical page of typescript after copy-editing.

carefully you have checked your typescript, some error of fault will
inevitably have slipped through.) Bearing in mind the already explained
consequences of added or deleted characters, words, etc. you must
endeavour to make your corrections maintain the existing number of
characters. If you delete a word or phrase, see if there is not some
innocuous padding with which you can replace it. If you need to add
words search for something of equal length that can be deleted.

You may also be asked to answer typesetter's queries. (These will
be in the margin, ringed, and probably in green ink. If the answer to a
query is 'yes', cross out the question mark; if the answer is 'no',
delete the whole query and write the correction in the margin. Replying
'OK' can be ambiguous.) If you make any comments, keep them brief the
printer doesn't want to read an essay.

The proofs must always be dealt with quickly. Your Agreement may
allow you two or three weeks for proof-reading; you are likely to get a
phone call from your editor asking you to turn them round within days.
This is NOT the time to send the proofs to a colleague for an opinion.
Burn the midnight oil; get them right and do it quickly.

You may find this proof-reading check list helpful:

o   Have you answered all the printer's queries?

o   Are all your author's corrections essential not merely cosmetic?
    (Be particularly chary of changing punctuation marks)

o   Have you used standard proof-reading marks?

o   If you have provided corrections, explanations or notes for the
    printer are they absolutely clear, legible, and brief?)

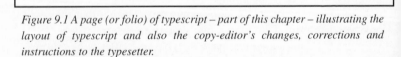

*Figure 9.1 A page (or folio) of typescript – part of this chapter – illustrating the
layout of typescript and also the copy-editor's changes, corrections and
instructions to the typesetter.*

Proofs

Once the copy-editing is complete – and hopefully checked by you – the marked-up typescript goes off for typesetting. Eventually – and it always seems a long time – you will receive a set of proofs for correction. With the proofs you may also get the original marked-up typescript.

In the past, proofs were produced in a two-stage process: first there were galley proofs and then later, page proofs. Galley proofs were long sheets of poor quality paper containing the whole book – but without illustrations (sometimes even without headings) and not split up into pages. Page proofs came later – hopefully with the galley proof corrections made – for further checking. Page proofs – both then and now – reflect the final appearance and pagination of the book. Nowadays, it is customary to omit the galley proof stage: you will almost certainly receive numbered page proofs – usually on poor quality A4 paper, but with page borders indicated. Actual illustrations may not always be included in the page proofs – but space will have been left for them.

Galley proofs are only used nowadays for the more complicated of 'technical' non-fiction books, where page layout needs extra attention.

Proofs are produced so that the layout and typesetter's work can be checked. They are not a means whereby you can improve your descriptions or explanations; nor are they an opportunity to change your mind. This point is so important that it warrants emphasis:

PROOFS ARE FOR CORRECTING – NOT FOR MIND-CHANGING

Even though today virtually all typesetting is done on a computer, minor alterations – a single letter or punctuation mark – may mean moving a word down a line. In turn, an added or deleted word can affect a whole paragraph or even where a page-break comes. It can generate unsightly 'widows' or 'orphans' – single, sometimes short, lines at top or bottom of the printed page. It could even, in a worst-case scenario, lead to the need for an expensive whole extra page.

Your prime task in checking the proofs is to seek out typesetting errors: mis-spellings, repeated, missing or incorrect punctuation marks, letters, words, lines or whole sections of text, wrong fonts (italic instead of roman, for example, or the reverse), or incorrect heading 'weights'. Watch out too for incorrect or missing running heads (if used) and chapter titles incorrectly repeated on the Contents page (such as different use of capital letters). Are all of the illustrations included – or space left for them? You will also now be able to – and must – correct the previously unknown page numbers that you showed in the typescript as '00'.

When proof-reading, take extra care. Because you wrote the book and know its content backwards, there is a danger that you will not read it carefully enough to spot the errors.

You can do the proof-reading on your own, as many authors do; you may find it easier if you can enlist the help of someone else. Whoever does it must note that the marking of errors requires the use of standard notes and symbols.

The standard symbols (from British Standard BS5261: Part 2) can be found in the annual *Writers' & Artists' Yearbook* and elsewhere – or the publisher may provide you with a copy. It is particularly important that not only are the errors marked in the text, but also with the appropriate mark in the margin. (The correcting typesetter checks only the margins for errors: no marginal note can mean an error going uncorrected.) Use two different coloured inks: red for correcting printer's errors, and black or blue for author's corrections. The printer will not charge for correcting his own mistakes but will certainly charge the publisher for all other changes.

There will be a clause in your Agreement to the effect that the publisher will deduct the cost of excessive author's corrections from your royalty account. 'Excessive' is measured as a proportion of the cost of original typesetting; error-corrections cost many times more than straight typesetting. Keep author's corrections to an absolute minimum to avoid being surcharged.

Despite the warning above, about only making corrections, not changes – and the costs – you must not allow your own errors of fact to remain uncorrected. (Murphy's Law guarantees that no matter how carefully you have checked your typescript, some error of fact will inevitably have slipped through.) Bearing in mind the already explained consequences of added or deleted characters, words, etc., you must endeavour to make your corrections maintain the existing number of characters. If you delete a word or phrase, see if there is not some innocuous padding with which you can replace it. If you need to add words – search for something of equal length that can be deleted.

You may also be asked to answer typesetter's queries. (These will be in the margin, ringed, and probably in green ink. If the answer to a query is 'yes', cross out the question mark; if the answer is 'no', delete the whole query and write the correction in the margin. 'OK' alone can be ambiguous.) If you make any comments, keep them brief – the printer doesn't want to read an essay.

The proofs must always be dealt with quickly. Your Agreement may allow you two or three weeks for proof-reading; you are likely to get a phone call from your editor asking you to turn them round within days. This is NOT the time to send the proofs to a colleague for an opinion. Burn your own midnight oil; get them right and do it quickly.

You may find this proof-reading check list helpful:

● Have you answered all the printer's queries?
● Are all your author's corrections essential – not merely cosmetic? (Be particularly chary of changing punctuation marks.)
● Have you used standard proof-reading marks?
● If you have provided corrections, explanations or notes for the printer are they absolutely clear, legible, and brief?)
● Have you 'corrected' all page, illustration or chapter numbers in references? Also on the Contents page.
● Have you balanced any deletions and additions with near equal additions and deletions?
● Have you checked for missing or repeated lines and passages?
● Are all illustrations acceptably located and do their numbers and the text references to them agree? Check the captions too.
● Are the running heads present, correct, and on the correct page – book title on left (*verso*) chapter title on right (*recto*)?
● Do chapter titles – and heading titles if included – on the Contents page agree with those in the text? (Check capitals particularly.)

You should have been sent two copies of the proofs – one set for your retention. Before you return the corrected set, mark up your own copy to match. You will use these to complete the index – *see* below.

You will not, usually, be the only person checking the proofs. As implied above, the typesetters will certainly have checked them themselves, generating the aforementioned queries. Almost certainly your editor will also have read them – or had them read by a freelance – and made her own corrections. When your corrections reach the publisher's office, they will be collated with the editor's/freelance's for returning to the printers. The editor may override some of your suggestions – and probably won't bother to let you know.

Completing the index

If you followed my recommendations in Chapter 8, your index is already half-done. Now that you have the page proofs it can be completed. Referring to your colour-marked file copy of the original typescript, mark up the page proofs to match – again, using colour for speedy identification. You will end up with all the index items colour-marked in the page proofs.

Now, with both typescript, proof copy and the draft typescript-page-numbered index all before you, correct the index entries. Start on page 1 of the page proofs and work slowly through; as you come to a colour-marked word or phrase, check it against the same colour-marked word or phrase in the typescript; look up the entry in the draft index – and 'correct' the page number. I suggest that you physically cross out the typescript page number and add the proof page number above or alongside. When you reach the last page of the proofs, the index should be completely 'corrected'. Check for un-crossed-out typescript page numbers – and find the missing proof-page references.

From your corrected draft index, either insert the proof-page numbers in ink on the 'top copy' typescript – or amend your copy on the word processor file and print out finished index sheets. The whole 'correction' process should take no more than a few hours.

The other way of producing the index is to wait until you have the page proofs and then start from scratch, exactly as in Chapter 8 but working directly on the page proofs. The advantages of the recommended method are the time saved at proof stage and the editor's awareness of the space needed for the index.

Most of my indexes have no more than 350-400 entries. Sometimes the index is even simpler, listing only magazine titles or the like; these are, of course, even easier to do. But some books, particularly the 'storyline' type, may need much more comprehensive indexes: names of many people and places, book and magazine reference titles, etc.

For more complicated indexes there are two possible solutions: employ a professional indexer (hopefully with the publisher meeting the cost, which will not be insignificant) or do it yourself using the index card system. For a professional indexer, approach the Society of Indexers – for their address, consult the annual *Writers' & Artists' Yearbook* (A. & C. Black).

The index card approach to indexing is to work through the book (at proof stage) preparing a small card for every identified index item (and a separate card for each secondary reference to the same item). When complete, arrange the cards in alphabetical order – and type the index directly from the cards. So far, I have never yet found it necessary to use this method – but it is undoubtedly favoured by some non-fiction authors.

It is unlikely that you will see proofs of the index itself; the editor herself will probably check it – there is seldom time at that stage for consultation.

The book arrives

All the processes that have been outlined in this chapter – editing amendments, copy editing, proof-reading and indexing – will have been spread over several months. But eventually, usually about twelve months after you delivered your manuscript-baby to the publisher, the book will be published.

The printer will deliver copies to the publisher about six weeks before the 'official' publication date. If you are lucky, you will receive your complimentary copies at the same early date. (The reason for the publication being some weeks after printing is to enable copies to be delivered to booksellers – and reviewers – in time for the launch.)

At last you have the first copies of your book in your hand.

Hopefully, you are 'over the moon' and delighted with how it has turned out. You read it through proudly . . . and almost inevitably discover a wee (unimportant) misprint that you didn't notice in the proofs. You wonder what the reviewers will make of the book.

As publication day approaches you grow more and more excited. But you are in for a disappointment.

Don't expect a champagne book-launch party – unless you're daft enough to pay for it yourself. Don't expect to be on a TV chat show. Don't expect a review in *The Sunday Whatsit*. Publication day will be awfully flat. If anyone phones to congratulate you or sends you a bunch of flowers – it'll probably be your live-in partner, or mother.

What to do with the complimentary copies? Depending on the publisher, you may be given anything from six to two dozen. If only six, take care what you do with them. All your friends – including some you'd forgotten – will want a free copy.

I always keep one copy of each book in pristine condition – hardly opening its pages; I call this my 'archive' copy. I keep another of the 'freebees' as my working copy; I refer to it frequently – and annotate it with amendments and notes for a possible second edition. If anyone has helped me with advice, comments, I usually give them a signed copy. And maybe a copy for your best friend, or your local library, or whoever sent you the flowers.

But celebration or not, you're now a published non-fiction author.

10

BUSINESS MATTERS

For the moment, the writing work is done. There's time now to stand back and take a look at some of the non-writing aspects that have been glossed over while we've been concentrating on producing your book: the business matters. They are important: they are part of the recommended professional – commercial – attitude to writing.

One of these important matters, already mentioned several times, is the Agreement. The Agreement is at the core of the recommended professional attitude. It is the contract between author and publisher, committing both to the project.

The Agreement

A whole book could be written about the details of publishing Agreements – but it would be of limited interest and potentially boring.

Most publishers have standard printed forms for their Agreements, with built-in provision for variation in some areas. Most publishers' Agreement forms are generally similar in most respects; many are based on a specimen contract produced by The Publishers' Association; some are negotiated with the Society of Authors and the Writers' Guild and incorporate minimum terms (the Minimum Terms Agreements, of which more below). The legal wording of the more-or-less standard clauses in a publisher's Agreement is appropriate to the businesses of publishing and writing; all that you will get if you ask your non-specialist High Street solicitor to check it for you is . . . a large bill.

Members of the Society of Authors (*See* Appendix 3) – you can apply to join as soon as your book is accepted – can have their Agreements professionally vetted by the Society free of charge.

The important thing about your Agreement is how it will affect you. You will usually have an opportunity to discuss the Agreement with your commissioning editor before the formal document is prepared. Even the standard printed clauses in the Agreement are not cast in stone; if you have a good reason for requiring the amendment of one of them, it can be done. Most – but of course, not all – publishers want to treat their authors fairly. For preference, sort out variations before the Agreement is sent to you.

The most important parts of the Agreement, to most 'ordinary' – as opposed to 'big name' – non-fiction authors are:

- the book length and delivery date
- the commitment to publish
- the royalty rates and advances

You will have told the publisher how long you expect the book to be; he will either have accepted that length or asked for it to be varied. However arrived at, with whatever compromise, you will both have agreed on a length. This figure will appear in the Agreement, committing you to deliver a book of that length. I have already explained the commercial importance of keeping to the agreed book-length. If you think you are under- or over-running you must discuss this with your editor who may suggest ways of achieving the agreed length.

Some Agreements specify the length in thousands of words (plus the number of illustrations); others in terms of book pages. Book pages can usually be translated at about 400 words per page – but remember to allow for the illustrations too.

The delivery date is as important as the length. You will have discussed this with the publisher: make sure you don't agree to a delivery date that you cannot meet; but a tight deadline is a better spur than the intermittent promptings of a supposed muse. The delivery date goes in the Agreement and you are committed to it. Again if, for a really good reason, you look like being late delivering, let the publisher know as early as possible. (You shouldn't deliver TOO early either.)

Both author and publisher are parties to the commitment to publish: you are committed to delivering a complete, *original* and *acceptable* manuscript (of the same standard and quality as the sample chapters), of the agreed length and on time; the publisher is committed to publishing the book (subject, understandably, to the effects of wars, strikes, acts of God, etc.) and to paying the agreed royalties. There is a clause in every Agreement whereby the author warrants that the material is original and does not infringe anyone's copyright, is accurate, is not obscene, blasphemous, etc. and that the author has not written and will not contract to write any competing works without the prior knowledge and agreement of the publisher. Another clause commits the publisher to publishing the book wholly at his own expense: often 'within a reasonable time' but better, 'within [a specific number of] months after delivery'.

But the best guarantee of all of the publisher's commitment is his enthusiasm . . . and the size of the advance that he has paid against your future royalties. (He will want to recoup his expense.)

To some authors, the contractual emphasis on the acceptability of the delivered manuscript is worrying. And undoubtedly an unscrupulous publisher might use this clause as an excuse to break the Agreement. But most publishers are not unscrupulous and as long as the delivered manuscript is up to the standard and promise of the synopsis and samples – coverage, accuracy, style, etc. – problems are unlikely.

Royalties and advances

Now the money side – royalties and advances. A royalty is a payment made to a book's author in respect of every copy sold; payments are not paid until after the copies are sold and accounted. Royalties are usually a percentage of the book's selling price. An advance is just that: an advance payment against as-yet-unearned future royalties; royalties are not paid until the advance has been recouped.

The financial arrangements for every book are unique though, and dependent on negotiation. Many publishers – at least initially – will offer a royalty rate of 10 per cent of the British published price for home sales of hardback books and $7^1/2$ per cent for paperback books. If there were such a thing, these rates would be the 'industry standard'.

Variations in the 'industry standard' are legion: mass market paperbacks sometimes only attract 5 per cent of list price; one specialist publisher of genre fiction pays only 4 per cent – but the sales are potentially huge.

Royalties for overseas sales and special deals – with book clubs, etc. – are differently based: usually 10 per cent of the net price received in respect of such sales. The author gets less per copy than for 'ordinary' sales – but so too does the publisher. That's fair.

Some publishers offer home sales royalties too, based on receipts. This simplifies their calculations. It also, unless compensated for, significantly reduces the author's – and only the author's – earnings.

Take the case of a hardback book selling in Britain at £10 per copy: a 10 per cent royalty based on list price gives the author £1 per copy sold; if based on net receipts the author will get at most 60 pence per copy – copies are commonly sold to the bookseller at a discount of around 40 per cent. A home sales royalty based on net receipts needs to be over 16 per cent to equate to one based on list price. (And a 40 per cent discount is far from the biggest on offer; for some bookselling chains, it can be over 50 per cent.)

An Agreement will often include provision for the basic royalty rate to increase when sales exceed a specified figure. This figure will depend on – but not necessarily be the same as – the sales needed for the publisher to recoup his whole initial investment. At the specified level, the royalty rate usually increases by $2^1/2$ per cent; sometimes there is provision in the Agreement for a second $2^1/2$ per cent increase in royalty. But don't hold your breath: many books never sell sufficient copies to reach the royalty jump figure. If and when they do, that puts the jam on your bread.

Royalties are usually paid once or twice a year – and customarily three months after the period on which they are based. (A very few publishers account for – and pay – royalties monthly for the first six months after publication.) If royalties earned do not exceed the advances paid, you will get an account but no cheque. If the royalties earned are less than a certain figure (nowadays, often £20) payment may be held over to the next accounting period. The annual accounting periods and payment dates are specified in the Agreement.

Authors should always ask for, if they are not immediately offered, a payment in advance and on account of future royalties. Most publishers will not object to paying an advance – but 'royalty-only' deals are no longer uncommon. Payment of the advance offers the author a partial surety for publication.

Unless they are a big 'name', non-fiction authors – of either 'technical' or 'storyline' type books – should ignore news stories about the massive advances paid to bestselling novelists. A few novelists are paid six- or seven-figure advances; most novelists are paid considerably less. So too are nearly all non-fiction authors. Few publishers would offer much less than a £500 advance nowadays (except perhaps for children's non-fiction); a £2000 advance for a 'non-name' 'technical' type non-fiction book would probably be generous. 'Storyline' type non-fiction books tend to attract the larger advances.

A first-time non-fiction author may have little idea of how big an advance to expect. One rule of thumb suggests that a middle-of-the-road advance should be half the royalty earnings of the initial print run. Thus: a conservative expectation of the advance for an £8 paperback on $7^{1}/_{2}$ per cent royalty and a 2000-copy print run would be:

$$^{1}/_{2} \times 2000 \times 0.075 \times £8 = £600.$$

It is a reasonable assumption that if a publisher pays you a larger-than-usual advance, he will push harder to achieve the sales that will recoup his larger-than-usual expenses. There is also the 'bird in the hand ...' justification for the author pushing for as large an advance as can be negotiated. Ask. They can always say no.

Bear in mind too that the advance may be all you get. Not all books sell sufficient copies for the earned royalties to exceed the advance. The author's safeguard is that the advance is – certainly by the time the book has been delivered and accepted – non-returnable.

The advance is seldom all paid 'up front'. It is usually paid at any or all of the following points:

● on signature of the Agreement

- on delivery (or acceptance) of the complete manuscript
- on publication of the book

Better known or more experienced non-fiction authors can hope for the advance payments to be 'front-end-weighted'; new authors must expect less on signature and delivery, and more on publication – once all the post-delivery work is done. And there is only one advance: the stage payments are merely portions of the overall figure.

Not all non-fiction books are commissioned on a royalty basis, although this is vastly to be preferred (by the author). Some publishers and some sections of the publishing industry – including some children's non-fiction publishing – work solely on the basis of lump sum payments to the author. (This puts the author on the same footing as, for example, the illustrator.) Book packagers too often work on a lump sum fee basis.

If you are offered the choice of lump sum payment or royalty-based Agreement it is almost always best – a 'good bet' – to opt for the royalty system. But you will seldom be offered the opportunity to choose. The disadvantage of a lump sum payment – even if it's generous – is that if the book becomes a major commercial success, the author will have no share in its success. The choice is usually a lump sum payment or no commission at all. I will always settle for the lump sum – it's that 'bird in the hand . . .' thing again.

Other Agreement clauses

Some other clauses in the Agreement are also of interest, but perhaps of less importance, to the non-fiction author. Points to note include:

- You will be expected to indemnify the publisher against any infringement of copyright by you. (This has been discussed in Chapter 2.)
- You will be expected to meet the cost of excessive author's corrections – that is, if the cost of making the corrections exceeds a percentage of the original typesetting costs. (This has been discussed in Chapter 9.)

- You will be given a number of free copies of your book – seldom less than six, seldom more than two dozen – and will be allowed to buy further copies at trade discount; these are supposedly 'not for resale', which could compete with the bookselling trade; in reasonable quantities, though, a blind eye is usually turned. (Seldom mentioned in the Agreement, but you can usually buy one-off copies of the publisher's other authors' books at the same trade discount – which can be very useful.)
- You will often be expected to offer your next book to the same publisher – usually on the same terms. Many established authors hold that this clause should be deleted on the grounds that it offers the author nothing of value: the publisher can always refuse, and your work may be more valuable after a successful first book. Against that, it gives the beginning author at least one place to offer the next book. On balance, I would accept the clause, qualified to 'the next book *of the same type*' and 'at terms to be mutually agreed'.
- There will be clauses about subsidiary rights. These are some-times of considerable importance: you will know if this is likely. A strictly UK-oriented 'technical' type of book is unlikely to be of much interest elsewhere; the right to republish a successful 'storyline' type book abroad or re-issue it in a book club or paper-back edition might well be sought – and you will receive a pro-portion of the proceeds therefrom. In the first situation there is not a lot to worry about; in the second, however, the advice of the Society of Authors or the services of a literary agent may be help-ful. I have yet to be approached with an offer for the film rights of any of my non-fiction books. (Offers c/o A & B please.)
- There will be a clause dealing with the termination of the Agreement. You may think this is of little importance but you are wrong. Eventually, your publisher may well decide that (even) your book has run its course and will let it go out of print. The termination clause should enable you to ask for – and be granted – the reversion of the publishing rights in the book. You can then, perhaps, offer the book for republishing elsewhere, as a new edition. (This can be a realistic proposition: it has been useful to me.) The author should not have to pay anything – such as the balance of any unearned advance – for the reversion of the rights.

● There may be a clause authorising the publisher to withhold payment of part of the early royalty earnings (often 25 per cent) against the likelihood of unsold copies being returned by booksellers. This withholding will be for a specific period – a year or so.

Always remember: even though the document is printed and may appear immutable, many of the clauses in a publisher's Agreement can be changed – if the author pushes hard enough. If you don't like a clause, discuss it – and maybe ask for it to be changed. The worst you can get is a no.

The Minimum Terms Agreement (MTA)

The Society of Authors and the Writers' Guild of Great Britain have for several years been seeking to persuade publishers to amend the 'standard' terms to favour the author more. The Publishers' Association declined to assist and negotiations are therefore proceeding piecemeal with individual publishers. Several publishers have now signed up with the Society and the Guild along the lines of the MTA; an up-to-date list of signatories can be obtained from the organisations. Not all publishers who have signed up to the MTA have agreed the same terms.

The MTA seeks to reach – but does not always achieve – agreement on such matters and terms as:

● a limit (10 years perhaps, with provision for extension) to the period for which the Agreement is valid;
● once the advance has been 'earned out', no delay in passing on earnings from subsidiary rights, etc.;
● the author to be told the size of the print run. (In the past many publishers have been amazingly secretive about such matters.)
● the author to be involved in consultative discussions about the book's jacket/cover, blurb, illustrations, publicity and publication date. (But 'being involved' does not mean that the author will have a right to decide, or a veto; the publisher will often listen

. . . and then decide no. It is not unreasonable for the publisher to retain this prerogative – his is the financial risk.)

● no alterations should be made to an author's typescript without the author's knowledge – and agreement;

● minimum royalty rates and 'jumps':

hardback	– 10 per cent of list price for UK sales or of publisher's receipts from overseas sales on sales up to 2500 copies
	– 12 1/2 per cent ditto to 5,000 copies
	– 15 per cent ditto thereafter
mass market paperback	– 7 1/2 per cent of list price on home sales up to 50,000 copies
	– 10 per cent ditto thereafter
	– 6 per cent of published price on all overseas sales

● minimum percentages to be paid to author for sale of subsidiary rights – for example:

American rights	85 per cent
Translations	80 per cent
Quotation rights	60 per cent

The royalty rates which the Society and the Guild seek to negotiate are not necessarily applicable to some specialist and/or highly illustrated books.

Agents

With all these apparently complicated clauses and wished-for clauses in the Agreements, should you employ a literary agent?

Undoubtedly, an agent can sometimes persuade a publisher to offer better terms to an author. The author, negotiating his or her own terms will always be worried that if pushed too far, the publisher will just drop the project and walk away. An agent will usually negotiate more skilfully – knowing better the limits to push to.

Agents can also sometimes 'feed' a non-fiction author with work. Agents often know what new series publishers are planning; they also know the individual skill areas of their authors; it is part of their role to bring the two together.

Unfortunately agents are not always happy to take on non-fiction authors as clients. Agents make their living by taking a percentage – usually 10 per cent, but the figure is creeping up to 15 per cent – of all the (literary) earnings of their clients. Agents like big earners or good steady earners. Few non-fiction authors – particularly those writing in the 'technical' field – earn really large sums from their writing; few write enough books to become 'good steady earners'. Some 'storyline' type non-fiction authors of course earn big money; they need the services of, and will usually be welcomed by, an agent.

Similarly, if you are going to write a real blockbuster in the 'technical' type field – *How to Win Friends and Influence People* or Samuelson's *Economics* – an agent will be extremely willing and able to take you on, and will probably make money for you. But if you are going to write *How to Write Non-fiction Books* or *The Compleat Widget* or the like, you don't really need an agent . . . and would be hard pressed to find one willing to take you on.

The publisher's questionnaire

At some time, while you are writing your book, the publisher may send you a questionnaire. (Not every publisher uses such questionnaires; it is common practice, though, among the publishers of the more academic 'technical' type books.) The purpose of this long – and often frightening-looking – document is to help the publisher sell the book to booksellers and the public. It helps with sales promotion and publicity. It is in your best interests to be as helpful as possible. After all, who knows your book better than you? (Not even your editor.)

Typical of the questions/requests in such a questionnaire are:

- Describe in detail the reader(s) you had in mind while writing the book. Specify the reader's job and responsibilities or his detailed interests. Specify also the magazines most appropriate to his job or hobby. (Easy – we did all this when defining our target reader in Chapter 3.)
- Describe your book in a *single sentence*: say what it will do and for whom. (This may be tricky, but it's essential. Work at it.)
- Describe your book in about 200 words, as you would explain its relevance to a potential reader. (This will have been included in your sales package – Chapter 3.)
- Explain the ways in which your book meets a previously unmet need. (Again, *see* your sales package.)
- List competing books and explain how yours differs from them. (Sales package again.)
- List the magazines, particularly the specialist ones, likely or prepared to review the book. (Reviews – and, so the saying goes, even bad ones – are usually of more sales value than advertisements. Certainly one of my early textbooks was badly slated – unreasonably, of course – in a review, but sales were good, and held up well.)
- Can you suggest any well-known people in your field who might be willing to read your book in advance of publication – and endorse it for publicity purposes? (A cover-quote from a 'name' often boosts sales.)
- Describe yourself, and your particular credentials for writing this book, in about 200 words.

And, if the book is a textbook . . .

- Specify all of the examination syllabuses at which your book is aimed and how well each is covered. (If the book is syllabus- or examination-directed, it MUST meet those requirements.) Suggest educational bodies and institutions that might use your book.

Your answers to the questionnaire will be part of the briefing of the sales force; they may not (probably won't) read the book itself – but they will quote your answers widely, *sounding* knowledgeable.

The questionnaire will also often be referred to when the book's blurb is written.

The blurb

The blurb is the immediate and ever-present sales pitch at the potential book-buyer. It is the description on the back cover of a paperback or on the jacket of a hardback book. It has to explain just what the 'technical' type of book will *do* for the reader, what it's all about; it has to give a taste – that all-important flavour – of what's in store for the reader of a 'storyline' type of book. It has also quickly to establish the author's credentials. Its importance can hardly be over-emphasised; it may be all that's read – or it may lead to a sale.

There are considerable skills entailed in writing a successful blurb. It will usually be written by someone fairly senior in the publisher's editorial team – in consultation with the sales manager.

Much of what's in the blurb will come from material the author has provided – either in the aforementioned questionnaire or in answer to a specific request for a biography, for instance, or in discussion. Occasionally, a non-fiction author may be invited to produce a draft; they will often be invited to check or factually approve what someone else has written. The author will seldom have the last word though – it has too important an influence on sales-to-come.

Against the possibility of being asked for a draft blurb for your book, study the blurbs on up-to-date competing and similar books. For 'technical' type books, blurbs can with advantage use bullet-point lists – listing how the book will help or improve the reader. And, while it is important to avoid suggesting that the book contains or will do something that it doesn't, it is essential not to play down what it does offer.

For 'storyline' type books, the blurb needs to be more literary, more 'continuous', describing some of the more important occurrences that the book deals with. (Bullet-point lists are not appropriate.)

But whether 'technical' or 'storyline' book, keep the blurb down to 200 words.

The author's biography, which customarily appears adjacent to the blurb, should always, for all types of book, be short – 50 words is about right – and relevant to the book. If the book is about your hobby no one wants to know much about your day-time profession or your domestic arrangements. The biography should laud your achievements in widget-collecting or rock-climbing or whatever. It achievements in widget-collecting or rock-climbing or whatever. It should outline your credentials for writing the particular book.

Whether invited to or not, it is worth trying to write a blurb and biog. for your book. Write the blurb particularly, early on in the writing period; you will find that doing so concentrates the mind – and will help the rest of the writing. And the biography's always useful.

The sales campaign

It is the publisher's business to sell your book: mainly, to booksellers; occasionally, direct to the reading public. You should be prepared to assist in the sales campaign and perhaps offer occasional suggestions – but don't try to teach the publisher his job.

The main sales effort will come from the publisher's sales force. There will be a team of representatives – sometimes in-house, sometimes contracted out – who will visit booksellers, seeking sales. The sales force will not be selling your book alone; they have a whole range of books to offer the bookseller – and all in a relatively short time (minutes rather than hours). It is because the reps have to 'make their pitch' in a minute or so per book, that they need the one-sentence descriptions and 'main selling points' from the publisher's questionnaire.

Many first-time authors are surprised when their book is not widely advertised. But few advertisements – except occasionally in specialist magazines – of general non-fiction books are cost-effective. Reviews of your book will be of greater benefit. Again, this is why the publisher will have asked for details of relevant journals.

There are never as many reviews as the first-time author expects though: the quality Sundays and daily broadsheets may review a 'storyline' book; they are most unlikely to review a 'technical' type non-fiction book. Even your local newspaper will probably ignore your literary masterpiece – unless they have an odd corner they need to fill up. Often, 'reviews' will be no more than half-a-dozen lines – and those copied directly from the blurb.

You should get a review in at least one of the specialist journals relating to the subject of your 'technical' type non-fiction book – but you'll have to wait several months to see it. Develop a thick skin too: not all reviews will be complimentary. You must hope that most are. (Console yourself with the show-biz saying that it doesn't matter what they say, as long as they get your name right.)

Some publishers will run a mail-shot campaign, distributing leaflets to a proven mailing list, seeking direct sales. Not all publishers will do this; it conflicts with the interests of the trade booksellers. Once again, this is for the publisher to decide, not you.

However achieved, sales should be high on publication; inevitably, they will fall off quite sharply soon after. The ideal non-fiction book is one that then settles down to a steady, not too small, sales level.

Having made the point that selling the book is the publisher's responsibility, there are ways in which the author can help. If you can write a feature article on a related topic, you can sometimes persuade a magazine editor to mention your book – and even include an illustration of its cover. If you hear of a seminar or evening class being run on a related topic, tell your publisher: he might be able to arrange a sales display. You yourself, now a published author (therefore 'an expert'), may be asked to give a (paid) talk: be sure to take along copies of your book for sale.

Book pricing

Sales do not depend solely on the efforts of the sales force; they are also of course a function of the book's price. If a book is, or appears, over-priced, sales will suffer; if priced too cheap, the publisher makes insufficient profit.

Many first-time authors, too, wonder about where the book-reader's purchase money goes – and how little the author seems to get. But book publishing is not the 'licence to print money' that some think. Let's look at how a book's selling price is made up.

Some years ago, Tim Hely Hutchinson, now chief executive of Hodder Headline plc, explained it all. In an article in *The Author*, the quarterly journal of the Society of Authors, in Autumn 1988 he gave a rudimentary breakdown of who gets what. Bearing in mind that

that different publishers have different ways of breaking down the costs and that they will vary from book to book, the breakdown in *The Author* was:

Booksellers' trade discount	50%
Manufacturing costs	17%
Publisher's overheads (including editorial)	10%
Distribution and marketing	8%
Author's royalties	10%
Publisher's net profit	5%

When viewed like this, the publisher is clearly no longer the ogre he seems to some. And if the booksellers' discount looks excessive, it is a fact of life: the major booksellers have to pay High Street rent and rates, and considerable staff costs and overheads.

Public Lending Right (PLR)

Still on money, the annual distribution of Public Lending Right earnings is an important source of earnings for the non-fiction author.

Each time a book is borrowed from any British public library, that loan is recorded. (In fact the loans are registered on a regularly changing sample basis and grossed up, but the principle is the same.) The Government provides a variable sum of money each year which is then distributed to all authors whose books have been borrowed from public libraries during the past year. For a single loan the payment is small – just one or two pence – but when this is multiplied by the nationwide loan figure it can be worthwhile. (In 1995 there were more than 24,000 registered authors; about 5,000 authors received no payment at all, 14,000 earned under £100; about a hundred authors earned the maximum figure of £6,000 – earnings above £6,000 are not paid.)

As soon as, but not before, your book is published you should register yourself and the book for PLR. Write to The Registrar, PLR Office, Bayheath House, Prince Regent Street, Stockton-on-Tees, Cleveland TS18 1DF for registration application forms and full details.

Managing your writing income

Whether you write just one book or go on to write many more, you must keep account of your earnings and expenses. Expect a demand for income tax on all your book-writing earnings. If you keep note of your expenses – including those incurred before your book was published – these can be set against the earnings and reduce your tax liability.

This accounting need not be a major exercise. A simple record of all receipts and all expenses in a cash book will suffice – at least initially. (Once successful, it may be worth seeking the services of an accountant; there are some who specialise in writers' problems.)

For my own interest I like to know where my expenditure is going; I record all expenditure twice – once as a straightforward outgoing and then again, by category. I classify expenditure under headings:

- postage (always a major expense)
- research (cost of photocopying, specialist books, etc.)
- stationery (it mounts up)
- travel (ticket costs, or cost/mile for car travel)
- others (telephone charges, attendance at conferences, etc.)

Such a breakdown lets me more readily explain and justify my expenses to the tax inspector. Remember: tax avoidance is permissible, but tax evasion is illegal. Never falsify expense claims.

Future work

Your book is published and copies are in all the shops. What now? Are you a one-book wonder or have you caught the writing bug? Maybe you're already thinking of the next book you'd like to write?

That's fine – and not unusual . . . as long as you have the content in you. The writing bug is virulent. Go back to page one of this book and start the process all over again – but now let your own experience temper my advice. This book has told you how I think it

128

should be done; if your experience suggests different – make changes. And good luck.

But you must also not neglect your first-born. You must keep up-to-date on its subject against the possibility of the publisher calling for a second edition. And here it is worth explaining the difference between an impression or printing, and an edition. If your book sells the whole of the initial print run, the publisher can readily print further copies of the original material, unchanged – or virtually unchanged. (Minor errors can be corrected.) This is a new impression or printing. When the book becomes out-dated and the text is in need of revision, this entails a second edition.

If you are required to prepare a new edition, be thorough. Do not merely add new material: out-dated material and out-dated thinking need removal; one or two chapters may need a total rewrite. At the same time, though, remember that it is a revised edition of the original book – NOT a brand-new book.

Good luck and best wishes for successful non-fiction authorship.

APPENDIX 1

THE NON-FICTION AUTHOR'S LIBRARY

Every non-fiction author will build up a comprehensive library of books in his or her specialist subject. That library will be unique to the author. But non-fiction authors can also benefit from a few books related to the writing and publishing process itself. The following list is by no means complete or exclusive; it is merely some of the books that I have found useful.

Reference handbooks

Writers' & Artists' Yearbook (A. & C. Black, annually)
The Writer's Handbook (Macmillan, annually)
    These two annual handbooks provide a vast amount of information, including details of hundreds of British and overseas publishers. But their vast coverage means only limited information about each. They also include a comprehensive listing of British and foreign magazines and advice on a whole range of matters of importance to writers. One or other of these handbooks should be on every author's bookshelf.
Gordon Wells: *The Book Writer's Handbook* (Allison & Busby, biennially)
    Much detailed information – contact names, method of approach, requirements, etc. – about fewer, carefully selected publishers.

The Concise Oxford Dictionary (OUP) – or a similarly comprehensive dictionary of your choice.
The Oxford Writers' Dictionary (OUP)
    Authoritative advice on preferred or 'tricky' spelling, when to use capital letters, abbreviations, punctuation, etc.
Roget's Thesaurus (Penguin)
    Inexpensive and useful – but resist the temptation to use unusual words.

Any comprehensive dictionary of quotations. (I have several, the main one was compiled by D. G. Browning for Everyman's Library, J. M. Dent. There are many other excellent compilations.)

Writing and publishing

Bill Godber, Robert Webb and Keith Smith: *Marketing for Small Publishers* (Journeyman Press)
> Eminently readable; explains how a publisher works. It's to everyone's advantage if the author understands what's going on.

Ann Hoffmann: *Research for Writers* (A. & C. Black)
> The classic. Near essential for all non-fiction authors – and particularly so for writers of 'storyline' type non-fiction books. A veritable mine of information and advice on how and where to research your book – written by a professional researcher.

Dorothy M. Stewart: *Bluff Your Way in Publishing* (Ravette Books – Bluffer's Guides)
> A pocket guide to publishing: hard facts interspersed with humour.

Writing style

Robert Gunning: *The Technique of Clear Writing* (McGraw-Hill, New York)
> Famous for inventing the Fog Index, Gunning has long been my guru. Follow Gunning's advice and your writing will always be clear and understandable.

Graham King: *Good Grammar in One Hour* (Mandarin/*The Sunday Times*)
> Free from jargon; easy to read; and lives up to its 'one hour' claim.

Keith Waterhouse: *Waterhouse on Newspaper Style* (Viking/Penguin)
> You may think that newspaper style is not wholly appropriate for a non-fiction author but this book contains more sense on writing style than any other I know. You can always skip the 'tabloidy' sections.

APPENDIX 2

A GLOSSARY OF PUBLISHING TERMS

A comprehensive glossary of printing and publishing terms would fill a book. (For instance, Martin H. Manser: *Printing and Publishing Terms* [a Chambers Commercial Reference book].) But even a limited awareness of some of the terms will help a non-fiction author to understand what the publisher is talking about. This minimal glossary should help:

advance information (AI) sheet: Promotional material, usually a single A4 sheet, giving bibliographical details and a summary of a forthcoming title. Circulated to potential buyers some months before publication.

ASCII (American Standard Code for Information Interchange) file: A computer file containing text in a form which can be read by virtually any personal computer. Most word processors will convert material into ASCII form: basically characters without formatting instructions.

backlist: A publisher's books published before the current season but which remain in print and available for sale.

blurb: The important promotional material relating to a book which appears on its back cover or jacket. It describes, in brief but glowing terms, the book's content and tells how the potential purchaser will benefit from the book. The blurb is also used in advertisements, etc.

bullet: A solid round dot (occasionally a square) used, as an alternative to numbers, to introduce items in a list.

copy-editing: The correction of an author's spelling, grammatical and punctuation errors before the manuscript goes for typesetting. Includes any amendments needed for compliance with the publisher's house style.

drop cap(ital): A large capital letter extending over two or more lines below; used at the start of a section of text.

dues: Orders placed for a book which is not immediately available, and are recorded for later supply.

em (also known as a *pica*)**:** A printer's unit of measurement based on the size of the letter M. An em is the square of any size of type – thus, a 10-point em is 10 points wide. The 12-point em is the standard measure of typeset material. Also, the *em-rule* – a dash, one em in length.

en: Another printer's unit, the en is half an em wide. Also, the *en-rule*, a dash, half an em long, used for time-periods, eg. 1989–95.

imposition: Assembling the book pages on a large sheet so that when the sheet is folded the pages will be in the right order.

imprint: Usually the name of the publishing house. But large publishers use various imprints – for example, Thorsons is one of the imprints of HarperCollins.

jacket: The protective paper sheet folded around a hardback book.

list: All the titles a publisher has in print and available for sale.

mail shot: a mailing of promotional material to potential customers.

Net Book Agreement: A now-abandoned agreement that books would not be retailed at discounted prices.

OP (out of print): No stock and no reprint envisaged.

orphan: The first line of a paragraph, isolated at the foot of a page.

perfect binding: Binding method whereby the signatures are trimmed to individual sheets, which are glued together, and to the book's cover.

pica: 12-point type, also another name for an em.

point: The standard unit for measuring type size. One point is the size of a pica full stop, 0.01383 inch (approximately 1/72 inch). 'Set in 10/12 point Baskerville' means that the typeface area is 10 points high, but the lines are set 12 (rather than 10) points apart, for greater ease of reading. Baskerville is a design of typeface.

range: To align characters or lines of text one below the other. Thus, 'range left and right' means the text is aligned at both margins.

running heads: The headings at the top of each printed page. Usually, the book title is on the left page and the chapter title on the right.

shout (or shout-line): A descriptive or complimentary statement about a book which appears on the cover, prominently displayed.

signature: A folded printed sheet, usually comprising 16 or 32 pages. All publishers will try to adjust a book's layout – by cutting words, or line-spacing, for instance – to fit into complete signatures.

subscription: Orders for a book received in advance of publication.

widow: The last line of a paragraph, isolated at the top of a page.

APPENDIX 3

WRITERS' ORGANISATIONS

Once your first non-fiction book has been accepted for publication and before you sign the Agreement, you should consider joining one or other of the writers' trade unions.

The Society of Authors: an independent trade union, not affiliated to the Trades Union Congress, and by far the older of the two trade unions, the Society has over 5,000 members. The Society caters for the needs of both fiction and non-fiction authors. There are various specialist groups within the Society for eg. educational writers, scientific writers, children's writers, etc. It produces an excellent quarterly journal, *The Author*, and a helpful but slightly frightening twice-yearly supplement, *The Electronic Author*. It has a small but efficient professional staff who will offer advice and guidance on all manner of authorial matters. The annual subscription is currently £65 (£60 if paid by direct debit).

Further information from The Society of Authors, 84 Drayton Gardens, London SW10 9SB. Telephone 0171-373 6642.

The Writers' Guild of Great Britain: a TUC-affiliated but non-political trade union founded in 1959, as the Screenwriters' Guild, to whom membership was initially restricted. In 1974, book authors and stage dramatists became eligible for membership. The Guild produces two newsletters for its members: one contains information 'From the Office'; the other, a quarterly, carries articles, letters etc. from members. The Guild's membership fees are £60 per year plus 1 per cent of an author's earnings from professional writing in the previous year.

Further information from The Writers' Guild of Great Britain, 430 Edgware Road, London W2 1EH. Telephone 0171-723 8074.

INDEX

INDEX